PRAISE FOR
THE EARLY CAREER BOOK

T0159906

"When I was a junior researcher, not even up, let alone coming,
people who were the age I am now used to give me advice. One was
'You have to be in the right place at the right time,' which is totally
useless – how can you know? And the second was 'The science will
speak for itself,' which was just plain wrong. Ever since then I avoided
giving any advice to anyone who finds themselves now in the position
I was all those years ago. Except one. Read this book."

PROFESSOR SIR SIMON WESSELY
FMedSci, FRS, Regius Professor of Psychiatry, King's College London

"This book is an invaluable roadmap of how to progress your career,
complete with tips for success, issues that trigger you, and traps to
avoid. It is written in a wonderfully conversational style – like talking
to your best friend spliced with evidence and insights drawn from
research and best practice. I really wish I had had something like
this when I was starting out."

PROFESSOR DAME ANNE MARIE RAFFERTY
Past President, Royal College of Nursing

FOR OTHER TITLES
IN THE SERIES...

CONCISE ADVICE LAB

SMALL BOOKS: BIG IDEAS

CLEVER CONTENT, DYNAMIC IDEAS, PRACTICAL
SOLUTIONS AND ENGAGING VISUALS –
A CATALYST TO INSPIRE NEW WAYS OF THINKING
AND PROBLEM-SOLVING IN A COMPLEX WORLD

www.lidpublishing.com/product-category/concise-advice-series

Published by
LID Publishing
An imprint of LID Business Media Ltd.
LABS House, 15-19 Bloomsbury Way,
London, WC1A 2TH, UK

info@lidpublishing.com
www.lidpublishing.com

A member of:

businesspublishersroundtable.com

© Rosie Duncan, 2024
© LID Business Media Limited, 2024

Printed by Severn, Gloucester

ISBN: 978-1-911687-94-8
ISBN: 978-1-911687-95-5 (ebook)

Cover and page design: Caroline Li

THE EARLY CAREER BOOK

YOUR GUIDE TO STARTING OUT, STEPPING UP AND BEING YOURSELF

ROSIE DUNCAN

MADRID | MEXICO CITY | LONDON
BUENOS AIRES | BOGOTA | SHANGHAI

This is dedicated to my daughter Calista,
who was born two weeks before this book was.

I want to say a huge thanks to my family
for their invaluable support, love and feedback.

CONTENTS

THE EARLY CAREER NAVIGATION SYSTEM   xii
INTRODUCTION   xiii

PART ONE: VALUES
1. WHAT ARE VALUES?   2
2. WHAT MAKES YOU TICK?   5
3. WHAT TURNS YOU OFF?   7
4. WHAT TO COMPROMISE ON   10
5. DEVELOPING AUTHENTIC VALUES   12

PART TWO: LIVING A VALUE-DRIVEN LIFE
1. VALUES VS. BEHAVIOUR   20
2. TAKING POSITIVE ACTION   22
3. WHAT NOT TO DO   24
4. YOUR PERSONAL MANIFESTO   26
5. CHECKING YOUR ALIGNMENT   28

PART THREE: GAME PLAN
1. THE POWER OF A PLAN   34
2. GOAL SETTING   37
3. MANIFESTATION   40
4. SELF-SABOTAGE   42
5. SUSTAINING ENERGY   45

PART FOUR: REJECTION AND RESOLUTION

1. HANDLING REJECTION   52
2. TRIGGERS   54
3. IS IT PERSONAL?   56
4. PERSPECTIVE   58
5. RESOLVING CONFLICT   60

PART FIVE: BOUNDARY SETTING

1. INTERFERENCE   66
2. OVERWORKING   68
3. ENERGY VAMPIRES   70
4. EMOTIONAL DUMPING   73
5. WORK DUMPING   76

PART SIX: FINDING YOUR STRIDE

1. ENTHUSIASM CYCLES   82
2. RECOGNIZING YOUR GOOD BITS   84
3. WORKING ON THE BAD BITS   87
4. COMMUNICATING HOW YOU WORK BEST   89
5. A HEALTHY ATTITUDE   91

PART SEVEN: HOW TO GET PROMOTED

1. MEASURE YOUR PROGRESS   98
2. BE KEEN   101
3. BE SEEN   104
4. BE HEARD   107
5. STAND OUT   109

PART EIGHT: WHEN THINGS GET TOUGH

1.	WHAT TO DO WHEN YOU SCREW UP	116
2.	BULLYING	118
3.	FEELING OVERWHELMED	121
4.	WHEN LIFE GETS IN THE WAY	123
5.	BEING HONEST WITH YOURSELF	125

PART NINE: STAYING OR GOING?

1.	YOUR JOY PERCENTAGE	132
2.	IS IT YOU OR IS IT THE JOB?	135
3.	WHAT WOULD CHANGE?	137
4.	RISK VS. REWARD	139
5.	NEW JOB DISSATISFACTION	142

PART TEN: CONTINUOUS SELF-IMPROVEMENT

1.	PERSONAL PROGRESS	148
2.	POSITIVE SELF-TALK	150
3.	HAVE A PANIC SYSTEM	153
4.	GET A SECOND OPINION	155
5.	THERE'S MORE TO LIFE THAN WORK	157

NOTES	162
BIBLIOGRAPHY	167
ABOUT THE AUTHOR	168

THE EARLY CAREER NAVIGATION SYSTEM

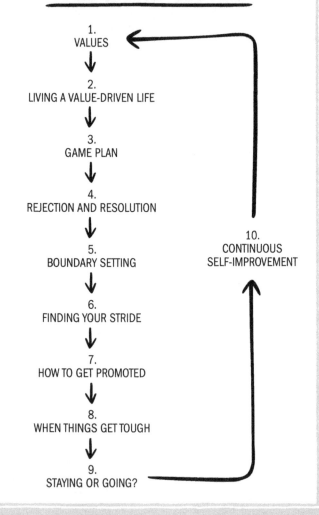

INTRODUCTION

We are taught many things at school, but 'how to handle yourself in the working world' is not one of them. Business studies and management courses teach you how to do things, but not how to deal with the politics and emotional aspects of working life.

We are thrown into a work situation where we hope that we have chosen the right job, have to deal with others in a professional manner, want to make a difference and strive to be seen.

There are, without a doubt, going to be hiccups along the way. You won't get on with everyone, you will be rejected at some point, you will make mistakes and you will have to motivate yourself on days when, quite frankly, you'd rather stay in bed.

This book is designed to set you up attitudinally to cope with all of this. To help you to work out what you'd like to do, set about getting what you want, know how to deal with rejection and learn from those moments, to set your boundaries, find your stride and get promoted, and to decide what to do when things get tough and you think about jumping ship.

I have been through every one of these moments myself, have had to make some brave decisions, and have ended up where I wanted to be. Here are all of the things I wish I'd known along the way.

Rosie Duncan
London, 2023

"

Working in line with your values will give you purpose and a reason to keep going on the low days.

"

VALUES

1. WHAT ARE VALUES?

WORK YOU VS. PERSONAL YOU AND WHY THEY SHOULD ALIGN

VALUES OVER MONEY

Money and status, until recently, were the dominant driving factors behind choosing a career. Nowadays we can add another key motivation to the mix: working in harmony with our personal values. In fact, to many of us, doing something that we believe in is even more valuable than the money we take home.

A 2021 Washington State University study highlighted that a massive 70% of Gen Z employees want to work for a company whose values align with their own, which accounts for nearly three quarters of those entering the workforce in the USA.[1]

BUT WHAT ARE VALUES AND WHY ARE THEY IMPORTANT?

Values can be defined as "the principles or moral standards held by a person or social group; the generally accepted or personally held judgement of what is valuable and important in life."[2] In other words, they are a set of standards that we each hold. Personal values are internal beliefs that align with our morals, and we use them as a compass to determine how we behave in our everyday lives. There are untold numbers of values that I could list as examples, but I'll start here: dependability, sustainability, compassion, collaboration and integrity.

If you get up most days and your work gives you a sense of purpose, joy and passion, it's a good sign that what you're doing sits well with you. On the flipside, if you are working out of sync with your values on a day-to-day basis, you will not feel motivated or inspired. You will be unlikely to feel pride in what you do. It's far more likely that you will see your job as unimportant, frivolous and potentially quite irritating.

COGNITIVE DISSONANCE

Cognitive dissonance is the internal imbalance or discomfort we experience when our words or actions do not align with our beliefs and values.[3]

It's important to work in an area that aligns with your values. Not only will it give you motivation to do your job, but it will also bring you a greater sense of satisfaction than the materialistic, superficial and finite realms that money and status bring.

Having purpose will give you pride in what you do, creating a self-motivating positive cycle where your pride fuels your passion, which in turn fuels your development and encourages you to do better, leaving you feeling rewarded and happy with yourself – or, in other words, proud. And here we are, back at the beginning of the cycle.

Working in line with your values will also give you purpose and a reason to continue on the low days. When things at work don't go your way – which, sorry to say, is inevitable – or you're doing that really boring admin task which *really* isn't something you enjoy, you can more easily accept your task because you know it is all for the greater good. Even when you are having a bad day or doing something that you deem to be tedious, you will still have a driving force spurring you on.

At the other end of the spectrum, if you aren't doing a job that aligns with your standards, you will not have the same motivation or sense of pride, and so will be less satisfied with your work. Given that we typically spend 40 hours a week (nearly half of our waking lives) at work, do we really want to spend that time being less satisfied than we could be?[4]

THOUGHTS AND RESOLUTIONS

2. WHAT MAKES YOU TICK?

WHAT MOTIVATES YOU?

So, now you understand what values are and why we want to work in alignment with them. But what are your values? What are your standards and morals? It's a really big question to ask yourself and you won't always know the answer straight away.

Some of our beliefs are inherited, whereas some are created through our experiences. It doesn't matter whether they come from nature or nurture. What matters is digging within and studying ourselves to understand what they are.

Self-study has been deemed important for thousands of years. *Svādhyāya* is a Sanskrit term that means 'self-study' or 'introspection.' It was written about and advocated as a key practice by Patanjali, an Indian sage, in the *Yoga Sutras* (dating to 200 BCE–200 CE).

Here is a starting point to get you thinking about what drives you:

MORAL VALUES

Some may be obvious. Perhaps you hold religious beliefs that have a set of morals to abide by, such as not harming others, or the importance of faith and dedication. Others may be more cultural, such as views on polygamous versus monogamous relationships. A way to investigate what you believe is to write down how you like to be treated and, just as importantly, how you *don't* like to be treated. For example, if you like someone to turn up on time when meeting you, it shows that reliability is an important factor to you. How do you like to be treated? How do you not?

MOTIVATIONAL DRIVERS

Here are some questions you can ask to uncover what your motivating values are. What are the things that get you out of bed in the morning? Are you a creative, an academic or a spreadsheet wizard? Do you enjoy public speaking? Are you motivated by money or doing good? What are your thoughts on the environment and diversity? (None of these options have to be mutually exclusive, by the way.) What subjects did you enjoy most at school, and why were they your favourites? What excites you? What do you hate?

Our values will change and evolve throughout our lives based on our experiences and the situations in which we find ourselves. So it's worth checking them every now and then if things have changed. Give yourself permission to evolve rather than locking yourself into a fixed, defined box that is hard to get out of further down the line.

3. WHAT TURNS YOU OFF?

THE VALUE OF KNOWING WHAT YOU DON'T WANT TO DO

Just as important as looking at what we like to do is looking at what we *don't* like to do. Ideally, we don't want to wake up every day dreading the tasks that we have on our to-do list. The more you dislike doing a task, the more onerous it becomes. It will stay stuck at the bottom of the to-do list and follow you around like a dark cloud until you decide to finally get it done. The more you delay doing it, the more dreaded it will become. In an ideal working situation, we want as few of these to-do-list burdens as possible.

It's helpful to use your dislikes as a springboard to determine what you do like. If you don't love presenting, perhaps because you are more introverted, do you instead like writing? Is that the ideal way for you to express yourself? This might mean that a job as a spokesperson isn't for you but writing the speeches to support a spokesperson is exactly your cup of tea.

So, what is it that you *don't* like to do? This can be a much easier place to start. We are often far more in tune with what we hate doing than what we like.

AVOIDANCE AND IGNORANCE

Sadly, we can't only ever do what we like doing. There are many situations where we have to do things we don't enjoy because they are essential. For example, few people enjoy sorting out their taxes every year, but it's essential to running a business. One way to tackle this is pure avoidance: ignoring it and hoping it will go away (which it won't) or shopping out the job to someone who does like it – in this case, an accountant.

But avoidance or handing the task over won't offer long-term behavioural change solutions. That is, you're going to continue to dislike doing the job whenever it might arise again in the future. What you should analyse is *why* you don't like these things to see if there is a pattern or an issue that needs to be tackled.

For instance, if you don't want to have a tricky conversation, it might be because you're not a fan of confrontation. The 'why' behind this could go as far back as your childhood. But you can't run from difficult conversations forever – sometimes these are pivotal moments in life. So how can you embrace being brave and set yourself some guidance to help with these moments? How can you turn this dislike into a positive trait? Knowing how you like to be treated in confrontational circumstances is a good template for you to know how to treat others when the same situation arises.

ADDRESSING YOUR DISLIKES

Sometimes, conquering your dislikes can give you a great sense of personal achievement and open a door to personal growth. Think about it. We often dread something because we don't have the skill set to feel confident about doing it. So the task at hand takes time and effort to undertake without being certain of the quality of the outcome.

But if you learn the skill that you need, and do it a few times so you know you're capable, you will have added another string to your bow and taken away the dread factor from a task you previously disliked. It may not become your new favourite item on the agenda, but your actions will most definitely temper your feelings towards it.

THOUGHTS AND RESOLUTIONS

4. WHAT TO COMPROMISE ON

WHAT ARE THE NON-NEGOTIABLES?

While it's great to dream big and have far-reaching goals, it's helpful to make sure they're achievable. You need to work within any constraints there might be and know what you are willing to compromise on. Don't fall into the trap of thinking that constraints are negative things. By knowing your limitations, you give yourself a smaller, but immensely powerful, space in which to play.

> "A constraint should be regarded as a stimulus for positive change – we can choose to use it as an impetus to explore something new and arrive at a breakthrough."
> (Adam Morgan, *A Beautiful Constraint*[5])

WHAT ARE YOUR CONSTRAINTS?

There are many types of constraint that you might be working with. Here are a few examples:

- **Geographical:** Where are you based? What is accessible to you? Are you able to work from home?
- **Physical:** What physical factors might influence your decisions, such as physique, physical abilities or working with dyslexia?
- **Mental:** Do you have any phobias or mental health related circumstances that will impact what works for you?
- **Financial:** What salary do you need at a basic level to cover your costs, and what would you ideally like to earn?
- **Historical:** What education or skills do you have? What are your strengths and weaknesses? Do you need to learn something new?

Now you have your list, are any of these negotiable?

Perhaps you would be willing to take a slightly lower salary if it meant that you could work from home and spend time with your loved ones, because you know – from working through your values – that family time is imperative to your happiness. Maybe you would be happy to move to a job in a different location because it offers the training you need to progress. You might be willing to drop your day rate to work in an organization that aligns with your values.

These factors will adapt as your life circumstances change and develop. But, for now, you are developing a good idea of what you're willing to compromise on and what are your non-negotiables – all vital information when you start job hunting.

5. DEVELOPING AUTHENTIC VALUES

HOW TO DEVELOP AND EXPLORE YOUR VALUES

By this point, thanks to your self-exploration, you should have a good understanding of your values. How many you have is up to you. Some schools of thought say that you only really have one key defining value, but it isn't helpful to put restraints on how many things you deem to align with you. The key point is that they should all feel real, authentic and instinctual.'

If you're still stuck as to what your values are, use people you admire as a source of inspiration. Take a look at role models, family members and people you follow, and ask yourself why you follow them. What is it that they do, or what spirit do they have that makes them so magnetic? What do you respect about them?

SENSE-CHECKING THE REASONS BEHIND YOUR VALUES

You may decide that there are values you would like to have, but don't currently. The first step is acknowledgement, followed by an interest to explore. Maybe you would like to be more ambitious but it doesn't come naturally to you. The first question, before trying to implement any behaviour change, is why don't you have that within you? Does it come from a desire to protect yourself or how you were brought up? We don't all need to have the traits that society deems important. If after some self-enquiry you'd still like to embrace this new value, think about what you need to learn or what behaviour changes (which we will look into more deeply in *Part Two*) you need to embody.

Here's an example that might help. I wanted to be able to reframe my naturally sensitive nature to become more emotionally robust in the workplace. I wanted to incorporate within myself the value of emotional stability when faced with uncomfortable moments. My self-enquiry went something along these lines:

As a highly sensitive person I had come to admire emotional stability in the face of criticism. But I would always be the one to cry when told I hadn't done well enough. I love emotions – I think they are brilliant – but in this case they were unhelpful because when I'm crying, I'm not listening. My thoughts are everywhere and I'm only thinking about myself. I realized that if I was able to listen to what was being said, I might be able to take on some constructive criticism and use that to self-develop, to discuss the matter further, or potentially even to defend my actions, rather than succumbing to emotional flooding.

In the most simple terms, **emotional flooding** is the experience of being overwhelmed when strong emotions take over, producing an influx of physiological sensations and an increase in the stress hormones adrenaline and cortisol. It often results in difficulty accessing our resources for calming down.

THE IMPORTANCE OF AUTHENTICITY

Without looking into the 'why' behind values that you want to develop, you'll find that enveloping them into your life authentically will be tough and feel jarring. The 'why' is important as it gives us our reasoning. It tells us about who we want to be. For example, if you're a man and you want to become emotionally stable because you have been told by society that 'men don't cry', on reflection you may deem this as the wrong reason to embody that value. So take time to investigate your why.

Where do your lists of values, constraints and non-negotiables leave you? What areas are you starting to settle on?

"

There is value in knowing what you don't want to do.

"

PART ONE NOTES

MY VALUES

WHAT MAKES ME TICK?

WHAT TURNS ME OFF?

WHAT ARE MY NON-NEGOTIABLES?

DEVELOPING AUTHENTIC VALUES

"

Integrity is an incredibly attractive trait to potential employers.

"

LIVING A VALUE-DRIVEN LIFE

1. VALUES VS. BEHAVIOUR

VALUES ARE BELIEFS;
BEHAVIOURS ARE HOW YOU ACT

ACTIONS SPEAK LOUDER THAN WORDS

It's a good place to be when you are clear on your values. But it's one thing to have values and another thing to act on them. Putting things into practice takes effort and energy. Without action, you're at risk of talking a lot about what you believe in but never actually embodying what you're saying – which could give you an unfavourable reputation of not doing what you say you will.

How you behave and carry yourself is a way of building up evidence that signals to those around you, and to yourself, that you are a certain type of person. Through the proof of your actions, you can hand on heart say that you are a living embodiment of your values.

HAVING INTEGRITY

Practising what you preach is what having integrity looks like. Quite literally, integrity means "firm adherence to a code of especially moral or artistic values."[6] This means that you set a code of conduct or values and live firmly by it.

Integrity is an incredibly attractive trait to potential employers. It means that you will deliver on what you say you will and behave in a considered fashion. And, if you have found an employer whose values align with your own, then the organization's behaviours and yours should match up, meaning you'll both be pulling in the same direction. Delivering on your promises will also foster trust between you both, which accounts for a huge part of a healthy working relationship – or any relationship, for that matter!

ALL TALK AND NO TROUSERS

You want to avoid becoming known as someone who talks a big game but never actually does anything about it. Here are a few reasons why:

- You will lose the respect of your colleagues. If they see that you aren't delivering on your rhetoric, they will view you as inactive and ineffective. What incentive or example does that set? If this snowballed to become an organization-wide way of working, it would create an organization full of many words but no actions.
- You will not make any tangible difference. Actions are what move things forward. Without actions, nothing changes and so everything remains the same. When it comes to securing a promotion, you need to show the differences you have made in your organization, which means showing your progress and the clear impact that you've had.
- You might as well not be there – which is a waste of your time and everyone else's!

THOUGHTS AND RESOLUTIONS

2. TAKING POSITIVE ACTION

HOW TO TAKE YOUR VALUES AND TURN THEM INTO PERSONAL GUIDING PRINCIPLES

You can now turn your values into a list of behaviours. You've talked the talk; now it's time to walk the walk.

Take each value you have written down so far. Now imagine how someone living with that value would behave.

AN OUTSIDE PERSPECTIVE

Looking at this from an outside perspective means you will pick out characteristics and traits that are visible from someone else's point of view, because that is how your behaviours will be projected into the world.

How would that person act if they valued, for example, self-development? The likelihood is that the person would spend time analysing themselves, look at what they needed to adjust and improve, and be curious to learn more. Being loyal may look like leaning in when a friend is having troubles and helping them through those tough times, rather than running away from the negative atmosphere of the situation because it doesn't feel good.

Here are some examples to show how values might manifest themselves as behaviours:

Value	Behaviour
Kindness	Being considerate
Transparency	Being honest and clear
Inclusive	Being aware of your biases and involving others
Environmentally conscious	Opting for eco-friendly choices

NOW IT'S YOUR TURN

The beauty of this is that there are tons and tons of ways in which 'kindness' (for example) might present itself as a behaviour – being considerate is only one of them. For you, this might be based on how others have been kind to you, or they might be influenced by your culture or by what your capabilities allow.

Use this as an opportunity to look at the differences in how a behaviour might play out and see which one appeals to you the most. Don't worry if it seems unnatural or uncomfortable to you right now. We will work through that together shortly. There is no set formula or instruction booklet. Take the opportunity to explore how this behaviour might work well for *you*.

3. WHAT NOT TO DO

WHAT YOU WILL <u>NOT</u> DO AND
HOW YOU <u>WON'T</u> BEHAVE

There's another (and potentially more fun) way to put your behaviours down on paper. As you did with your values, it is helpful to look at what you *don't* like to determine what you *do* like.

Here's a question: What do other people do that annoys you? What are your pet peeves? What annoys us can be much easier to reach for because it creates a visceral state of irritation that we remember.

> "Annoyance may well be the most widely experienced and least studied of all human emotions."
> (Joe Palca, National Geographic[7])

If you're anything like me, the answers to 'what annoys me' come rolling off the tongue. People walking slowly in front of me. People being late. Hypocrisy. The list could go on and on.

After the catharsis of writing this peeve list has settled in, you can turn it into something constructive. Let's start by taking the first two items in my list as examples.

MY PET PEEVE LIST
People walking slowly in front of me
To be clear, I won't be annoyed if the person isn't capable of moving quickly, but rather if they are on their phone, not paying attention or generally not noticing what's going on around them. Fundamentally, they are not being considerate to the other people on the street. The thing that is *actually* annoying me is their lack of awareness and consideration. So, being considerate is clearly a behaviour I regard highly.

People being late
This is not annoying if there is a genuine excuse and helpful communication along the way. It is only irritating if the person is nonchalant, doesn't update me as to their time progress and has no real reason for their lateness. To me, this says that they value their time more than mine. It boils down to a lack of respect for what my time is worth. So there we have it: I must respect people's time.

YOUR PET PEEVES
Now it's your turn. Take your annoyances and investigate why they bother you. Can you dig a little deeper to understand *why* they annoy you, thereby creating ground rules for your own behaviour?

4. YOUR PERSONAL MANIFESTO

CREATING A PERSONAL MANIFESTO BASED ON YOUR VALUES AND PRINCIPLES

A manifesto is a declaration of your beliefs and intentions. It lays out what's important to you and acts as a personal statement that expresses how you'd like to behave and what you'd like to gain from life.

Writing a manifesto is powerful. It can encourage you to consider what's really important to you, forces you to write that down in words, and acts as a constant reminder to stay true to yourself. When we have hard decisions to make, our manifesto can help us to decide the path that is most in tune with ourselves, even if it's the harder choice. It backs up our decisions because we know that we are living true to ourselves. It's hard to argue with that type of reasoning.

Your manifesto should make you feel powerful. It should give you goose bumps. It should act as an external backbone.

STARTING POINT

By now, you've explored the thinking behind your manifesto, which is 75% of the work. With your values and behaviours in mind, now write down in short sentences:

- What's important to you
- What you believe
- Who you are
- Who you'd like to be
- How you'd like to be known
- How you will act in order to achieve all of the above
- When things get tough you will always remember that...

You may want to reorder the points and play with the phrasing until each point sits right with you. Ideally you want your manifesto to be refined down to no more than a few paragraphs. This will almost certainly take a few attempts. You may want to try a first draft and revisit it at a later time to see if it still resonates. Don't worry about perfection – when it's 90% there, leave it as it is and allow it to live and breathe.

MAKE YOUR MANIFESTO VISIBLE

Make it your screensaver, write it out in your notebook, or print it and stick it on your wall. Every time you see it, you will be reminded of your purpose and vision.

THOUGHTS AND RESOLUTIONS

5. CHECKING YOUR ALIGNMENT

IS YOUR BEHAVIOUR IN LINE WITH YOUR VALUES?

If you look at how you go about your life now, does it sync up with your values? Let's reflect on your current behaviours. Start by writing out your actions on any given day. Be methodical. Start from the very beginning and go through the day for as long as you have the stamina. Write down even the most mundane activities.

Don't put this off. Why not do it tomorrow, noting down your activities throughout the day? Or now, reflecting on the activities you did yesterday.

Put what you've written next to your value system. Can you see your values shining back at you in how you are acting every day? Don't be alarmed if they don't. This is your moment to change that.

Granted, not every single action will reflect your values. For example, taking the kids to school would be deemed a necessity. But you will gather insight from *how* you do this. Are you always on time, demonstrating reliability? Do you always smile at the lollipop person, expressing your value for respect? Do you make an effort to talk to your kids on the journey and ignore your phone, showing that you value open communication by giving them your undivided attention?

HOW TO REALIGN YOUR BEHAVIOUR WITH YOUR VALUES

It might be time to update your behaviour. Don't panic – self-awareness and acknowledgement are the first step in any behaviour change, so you're already on your way.

Say you want to be more courageous. You need to start by thinking about how someone with that value would act. Then you need to start doing that yourself. Rather than creating big statements that might not be relevant to everyday life, such as "a courageous person wouldn't hesitate to run towards a burning building" (it's not that often we walk past burning buildings, after all), challenge yourself every time a relevant situation arises. An opportunity comes up that puts you outside your comfort zone. Instead of saying no immediately, ask yourself: What would a courageous person do? They would say yes.

It might feel odd at first, quite unnatural in fact. But by doing this, you will be building up an evidence base of actions showing that you are becoming the person you want to be. The more you do, the more you will prove to yourself that you embody the value and can say with integrity that you are courageous (or honest or kind or whatever value you are pursuing). And you will have the added benefit of knowing that challenging yourself will eventually become second nature as you create these new habits.[8]

You may find that the perfect time to start is when you meet new colleagues, because they will have minimal preconceptions about who you are.

PART TWO NOTES

DO I EMBODY MY VALUES?

MY VALUES AS ACTIONS

WHAT I WON'T DO

MY PERSONAL MANIFESTO

ALIGNMENT CHECK

"

Having a plan is the first step to success.

"

GAME PLAN

1. THE POWER OF A PLAN

WHY IT'S HELPFUL TO HAVE ONE

> "A goal without a plan is just a wish."
> (Antoine de Saint-Exupéry, *The Little Prince*[9])

We can have hundreds of goals, but unless we action them, they are simply unfounded statements about our intentions – or, as the writer Antoine de Saint-Exupéry rightly put it, they are just wishes. So it helps to have a plan to bring our goals to life: a thought-through structure that sets out a process and allows us to track our progress.

Having a plan is the first step to success, as the US Chamber of Commerce Institute for Organization Management acknowledges:

> "Research has determined that only 3% of all adult citizens
> in the United States take the time and effort to plan for
> the future. Yet, those 3% accomplish five to ten times more
> in their lifetimes than do the other 97%."
> (Chuck Ewart, US Chamber of Commerce Institute for
> Organization Management[10])

Some of the most successful people in the world start with a plan.
They don't just wing it. They are clear about what they want and,
just as importantly, they think through each step and lay out the
path to make sure it happens.

SELF-ACCOUNTABILITY

A plans acts as a roadmap. This means that on days when you're
feeling less energized and using your brain feels like a chore,
previous 'you' has already done the thinking part. You won't have
to turn your brain to bigger-picture thinking, which isn't always
easy when you're in the wrong frame of mind. Since you've already
thought things through, you simply have to enact the next step that
you've planned for yourself.

BE FLEXIBLE

Here's a thing to remember about plans – they change. It doesn't
matter if it's a six-month or ten-year plan, there will be things
along the road that mean you have to adapt. Life will most likely
get in the way. You might realize that you've changed your mind
and you don't actually like the path you have set out on now that

you've started it. You might digress completely because you realize there's another opportunity that's come about, or a topic that you want to spend more time on.

This is completely okay. You need to have flexibility for several reasons. If things aren't going exactly as you intended, you don't want to get into a cycle of mentally punishing yourself because you aren't on track. All that will do is make you feel bad and the likelihood is you will stop enjoying yourself and ultimately resent the path you've undertaken. You need to be honest with yourself when something isn't working and give yourself permission to course correct if you aren't happy with the original plan.

You should also stay alert to innovations and insights that are thrown up along the way. You may discover a golden nugget that changes your path. Famously, Sir Alexander Fleming didn't set out to create penicillin. He came back from a holiday to discover mould growing in his petri dish which was preventing the mould around it from growing. He then spent the next 20 years developing the world's first medicine that could kill bacteria.

THOUGHTS AND RESOLUTIONS

2. GOAL SETTING

TURN YOUR MANIFESTO INTO A PLAN

DECIDE ON YOUR GOALS

Arguably the hardest part of this is to decide what your goals are. But we need a point to aim for in order to know where we are going. So, when it comes to your career, what are your goals? Take a look at your manifesto and ask yourself these questions:

- Where do you want to be in five to ten years' time?
- What do you want to have achieved when you give up working?
- How would you like to refer to yourself when someone asks you what you do?
- Is the goal a financial target?

BREAK IT DOWN

Goals can seem incredibly daunting at first. When starting at £0, stating that you want to earn £50,000 in ten years' time can appear pretty unrealistic. It can seem so far-reaching that it puts you off trying to get there – in which case, you've already failed. This is why you will benefit from breaking your goal down into manageable steps – in other words, your plan. Psychologically, you are far more likely to achieve what you set out to by creating bitesize checkpoints along the way. And here's an example of how.

Start at the end and work backwards. What needs to be in place for you to be earning £50,000? What job could you be in? What does your living situation need to be? Does this type of money even exist in the career path you've chosen? Then take into account how many promotions you will need to get there. For each promotion, what will you need to achieve in order to step up? What might you need to learn on the way? What tactics can you employ to equip yourself with all the knowledge and skills you need to get there? Finally, where do you need to start – is it where you are right now?

And there you have it: a career roadmap.

SHARE WITH SOMEONE YOU RESPECT

Research from The Ohio State University explains that sharing your goals with someone higher up, specifically someone you respect, can help to motivate you. It keeps you accountable because once you have stated that you are going to do something, if then you don't do it, it could reflect badly on your character. And the fact that this is someone that you admire adds additional incentive because you want to impress them and not let them down.

"If you don't care about the opinion of whom you tell, it doesn't affect your desire to persist – which is really what goal commitment is all about."
(Howard Klein, Fisher College of Business, The Ohio State University)

THOUGHTS AND RESOLUTIONS

3. MANIFESTATION

MANIFEST WHAT YOU WANT ATTITUDINALLY

Do you have faith in your plan? Do you believe in your own ability to achieve your goals? A big part of the challenge is having the right attitude to see you through.

REVERSING NEGATIVITY

Unsurprisingly, not all of us are born full of confidence with relentless positive energy. In fact, nobody could keep that up all the time. Having negative thoughts is completely normal. According to Rick Hanson in his book *Hardwiring Happiness*, we have an in-built negativity bias that dates back to the Stone Age.[11] It exists to help us survive. Clearly, remembering the dangerous (negative) situations we have faced acts as a warning system for our future selves, meaning we will aim to avoid similar circumstances in the future, or at least have a better grasp of how to handle them. And the better prepared we are and the more we desire to avoid threatening situations, the more likely we are to survive.

The good news is that we can rewire our Stone Age brains to feel predominantly positive, which is more helpful for life today. You can create new neural pathways that, when used again and again, become habitual and automatic. One way to do this is to focus on positive experiences for prolonged periods of time. Even 10–20 seconds will help that experience to have a longer-lasting impact on your memory.

This is our first step to feeling positive about ourselves and our plan.

VISUALIZATION

There is a plethora of studies that investigate the power of visualization. Visualization is the act of imagining a situation and mentally walking through it in the way you'd like it to play out, before you actually encounter the situation. It's a common technique used by successful sports stars. Muhammad Ali and Tiger Woods are just two of many who use mental rehearsal to walk through events before they take place.[12] By doing this, we create mental instructions and practise in the same way that we would if we were physically enacting the situation.

Doing this makes the future less daunting. By imagining ourselves in a given situation, we create a virtual reality for ourselves that becomes increasingly defined the more we imagine it. We turn the fearful unknown into the known.

When looking at your goals, take a moment to picture what it would be like to have achieved them. Use all your senses. What environment would you be in? What smells and sounds would accompany that? How would you feel? Not only can you mentally visit your happy place, but you can also do so knowing it will help you get there.

4. SELF-SABOTAGE

HOW WE GET IN OUR OWN WAY
AND HOW TO OVERCOME IT

WHAT IS IT?

Self-sabotage is when we, consciously or unconsciously, get in our own way. We can do this in every aspect of our lives, especially in our relationships and at work. Below are some examples of self-sabotage – see if you recognize them within yourself. It's important to note that I have never known someone who doesn't self-sabotage on some level – so you are not alone.

- **Perfectionism:** Waiting for something to be 'perfect' before we share it with the world. This is a way to hold on to our work and never let it live.
- **Procrastination:** Doing everything *but* what you need to do, which leads to...
- **Last-minute panic working:** Who, honestly, does things better under pressure? This is far from the ideal working situation. If you give yourself the time needed, you can deal with things when they go wrong, have the capacity to change your mind and have space to develop your thinking.

- **Self-criticism:** Telling ourselves that we can't do it or that it won't be good enough.
- **Being disorganized:** Too much clutter and disorganization can increase stress. This increases our levels of cortisol – the stress hormone – which impacts our sleep quality and decreases our ability to rest and heal on both a mental level and a cellular level.

WHY WOULD WE DO THIS TO OURSELVES?

Some of us subconsciously choose to be in this state of self-sabotage, and for too many different reasons to mention here. Perhaps we *like* living in a negative space, because, by complaining, we generate attention, which is what we crave on a deeper level – wanting attention more than we want to succeed. Perhaps the fact that things never go our way is the only thing we can control in our lives, so we use this as a slightly perverse way to remain in apparent control of a situation. Perhaps we don't really want to get off our arses and do anything, so we try to prevent things happening before we are obligated to leave our sofas.

HOW CAN WE GET PAST THIS?

The online resource Positive Psychology has created a worksheet you can use to help you identify self-sabotage and change your behaviour when you notice it.[13] The link to the full worksheet is in the notes section of this book, but in summary, ask yourself these questions:

- How do you sabotage things in your life?
- Can you identify any particular patterns?

- How do you think self-sabotaging behaviours affect your well-being?
- What can you do differently?
- How can you commit to ending your self-sabotage?
- How will you reward yourself?
- What will you do when it's hard to stop self-sabotaging?

THOUGHTS AND RESOLUTIONS

5. SUSTAINING ENERGY

UNDERSTANDING YOUR
NATURAL ENERGY CYCLES

One thing that we don't often account for is that we all have natural dips in our energy levels. This affects how motivated we are. We have bouts of creativity, the sudden itch to clear things out and days where concentration doesn't come easily. With each surge, inevitably, the opposite sensation will soon follow.

It may surprise you to know that we can predict these highs and lows with some degree of certainty by thinking about the seasons, hormones and other factors. If we are aware of these patterns, we can arrange our lives to suit them, capitalizing on the highs and resting during the lows. If you predict a lower-energy state on the horizon, you may decide to not book yourself in to socialize with friends and opt to work from home (if that's an option for you). Or, if you know you'll be riding high, you might decide to take on an extra project.

Mentally, planning in this way means that we won't beat ourselves up so much when we're in a low state. Instead, we can accept it as a normal, and necessary, part of our human experience.

We're allowed to not be 'on' 100% of the time – in fact, it's not possible to be that way.

ANNUAL CYCLES

Every year holds work and seasonal cycles. Work cycles are influenced by school holidays, while seasonal cycles are dictated by the weather, which impacts how much energy we have to do things. In the UK, the year would look something like this:

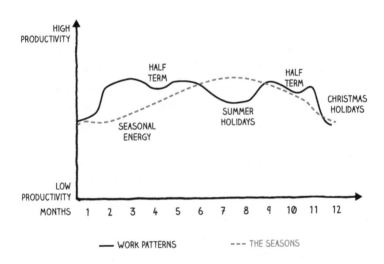

PERSONAL CYCLES

We all have our own personal energy cycles. Hormones affect both sexes, but I want to specifically mention how they affect the female members of our species as I feel this is an often overlooked, but vital, thing to understand. Menstrual cycles are taught about in schools, but the energy fluxes that come with that process aren't.

If you're a menstruating woman reading this book, I highly advise tracking your cycles to see where your energy levels and mental states are every day, especially around ovulation and when you bleed. You may find that it's not just your sleep and energy that are affected, but also how you feel – for example, in terms of your anxiety levels, your ability to be more resilient on some days over others, or whether on some days you have more of a pep in your step. The book *Wild Power* by Alexandra Pope and Sjanie Hugo Wurlitzer can help you do this.[14]

For any human being, learning about how foods, sleep patterns, days of the month and seasons in the year affect you will mean that you understand yourself much better. Start to be conscious of when things of note arise, see if you can spot a pattern and organize yourself around whatever it is that affects your energy cycles.

PART THREE NOTES

MY PLAN

MY GOALS

VISUALIZING MY GOALS

HOW TO AVOID SELF-SABOTAGE

MY ENERGY CYCLES

"
Our heads are
hardwired to
see rejection
as painful.
"

REJECTION AND
RESOLUTION

1. HANDLING REJECTION

WHY BEING ABLE TO HANDLE REJECTION IS SO IMPORTANT

THERE IS A REASON WHY IT'S HORRIBLE

We have all been rejected at some point, and let's face it, it's not a nice feeling. Rejections come in so many forms: not being invited to an event, being ghosted after a few dates or not getting the job you applied for. A University of Michigan study showed that when we recall rejection, the same part of our brain is activated as when we remember physical pain.[15] Put plainly, our heads are hardwired to see rejection as painful.

Evolutionary psychologists believe that this comes from a time when we needed groups to survive, since being alone in the wild would be a death sentence. So, as social beings we strive for community and connection, and it's natural for us to feel uncomfortable if we aren't accepted.

DON'T LET REJECTION BE THE REASON YOU DON'T PROGRESS

Rejection can be a powerful force, regardless of whether you learn how to handle it or let it go. The danger with rejection is that it could hinder your progression if you let it get to you. You don't want the fear of rejection to be something that you can't get past. You can't afford to become a victim of it in a way that stops you from ever leaving the house, trying to find a partner or going for the job you want. You need to find a way of getting over it so you can move on to the next thing.

It is inevitable that we will face rejection at some point, so we must learn how to handle it. Everyone does this in their own way, in their own time, and each experience is different depending on the severity of the rejection itself. You do not want to be the one holding on to bad experiences, letting them weigh you down, being constantly distracted by the past and, fundamentally, never getting on with what your future has to offer you. You can take these lessons and become stronger for them.

It's highly unlikely that you will get the first job that you apply for. You may even be fired at some point – I have! What's important is what we learn from the experience. This is easier said than done, but the next few sections offer some ideas.

THOUGHTS AND RESOLUTIONS

2. TRIGGERS

TRIGGERS

When we are facing rejection, it is usual for our emotions to be running high. The same can be said when we are dealing with conflict or any situation that puts us in fight-or-flight mode. It's often in these moments that we react before we think, and then come away feeling negative about the experience – angry, fearful, shameful or upset. These emotions can be caused by obvious shouting-across-the-room macro aggressions, or quieter micro aggressions – like being purposefully ignored (in comes rejection again).

At some point in your work life, you will encounter a situation like this. Rather than let these bad experiences taint your perspective, it's important to see whether there is anything positive you can take from them. There might not be. Just because you are attempting to be considerate, it doesn't mean that the other person is being anything but nasty. But, on the other hand, this may be a moment for growth by understanding what triggers you to respond in this way – and there is more often than not some 'good' we can take away, even if it's not that obvious at the time.

A TOOL FOR SELF-QUESTIONING

Let's imagine you are in a meeting and a superior critiques your work. Your initial reaction is likely to be instinctive and will depend on your character. You may shy away and say nothing. You may cry. You may defend your work. My advice here is, before you do anything that feels extreme, find a way to exit the situation.

Then, when you have had a moment to take stock, come back to what has been said. Break the situation down like this:
- What was it that upset you so much?
- Was it the way in which it was said?
- Was it the fact that it happened in front of other people?
- Was it that you weren't given any warning?
- Was it that the person had been nice to you up until this point and it felt like a betrayal?
- Was it that you were upset with yourself because you knew you weren't presenting your best work?

These are just a few suggestions; you can explore the situation for yourself.

What do your answers tell you? If you felt betrayed, you have to ask yourself why this matters to you. Maybe loyalty is high up on your values list. Separate yourself from this for a bit. Do you *need* loyalty from this person? Does this teach you about the person you work with and therefore how you can interact with them in the future?

Most importantly, what does this teach you about yourself?

3. IS IT PERSONAL?

WHEN FEEDBACK FEELS PERSONAL

Every job involves feedback – whether it's from our clients, customers or managers – and it's not always positive. Negative feedback can be a blessing in disguise because it is through the negative comments that we learn, grow and improve. But this doesn't mean that taking criticism is easy.

WHEN IT *FEELS* PERSONAL

A common response to negative criticism is to feel as though what's being said is personal. And if you're someone who cares what others think, this can really hurt. When we're hurt, we become offended and defensive and are less likely to listen to what's being said. We are instead consumed by our own thoughts and emotions.

In some cases, it's not just the content of the words being said, but the *way* in which they are said. Is it that the person's demeanour is triggering an emotional response in you because it reminds you of previous negative experiences? It may be that what was said was incredibly patronizing and that it really hit a nerve. If so, try to look past the tone and hear what was being said. Is there any value in what the person was *actually* saying?

WHEN IT *IS* PERSONAL

If, after some reflection, you decide you are being spoken to unjustly, you have two ways in which to view the interaction. One is with sympathy – there is a strong chance that the other person has had a bad day, or had bad past experiences, that are affecting how they are speaking to you. There is the option here to be sympathetic and enquire as to what, and why, this is happening. Turning our hurt into sympathy is a powerful and compassionate way to interpret a situation.

Sometimes, though, we don't have the emotional capacity to take the upper hand, or the comments coming our way are too hard-hitting for us to take a sympathetic route. At this point you can choose not to respect what is being said and who is saying it. As soon as you decide that you don't care about the other person's opinion, you take away their power. This might also be the time to work out how not to deal with this person again, if that is possible.

DON'T PERPETUATE THE CYCLE

It is our responsibility to give constructive criticism in a way that allows our colleagues to grow and that does not defeat their character. If things go south at work, passing the blame is not a wise or healthy thing to do. We will only maintain loyalty and contribute to a good team ethic if we refrain from finger-pointing ourselves.

4. PERSPECTIVE

THE POWER OF PERSPECTIVE

Having perspective involves taking a step back and reflecting on the situation.

DOES IT REALLY MATTER?

When something goes wrong, the first thing to ask yourself is this: Does this really matter in the grand scheme that is your life? In the moment, negative interactions are multiplied several times in our heads as they are emotionally confronting. Often, it's the negative stuff that takes up most of our brain space, whereas the positive stuff gets taken for granted and ignored (there is more on this in *Part Ten*). But, if you take a second and put the event into the broader context of what is really important to you, and the wider lens that is your life, does it deserve the time and attention that you are giving it?

THE OTHER POINT OF VIEW

You can give yourself a different perspective by considering what the situation is like for the person you are interacting with and why they might be behaving this way. This forces you to look at both sides of the spectrum and to input another – potentially very valid – point of view. By walking in the other person's shoes, you might start to understand their side of things and empathize better with them. Combine this compassion with a willingness to understand and you will start to create a constructive conversation where both parties are working towards compromise, rather than it feeling like a battle where no one moves forward.

THE POWER OF AWE

"Watch the stars in their courses and imagine yourself running alongside them. Think constantly on the changes of the elements into each other, for such thoughts wash away the dust of earthly life."
(Marcus Aurelius, *Meditations*[16])

You can also take a step back and consider the bigger picture. Nature is a great way to do this. Gazing at the stars or staring at the sea – or focusing on anything that inspires you to feel a sense of awe – will remind you that your experience is only one of the many that are out there, and that life is finite. Dr Julie Smith talks about how experiencing awe can help us to deal with anxiety. By feeling 'small', we can depersonalize the situation, which helps us to be grateful for what we have.

Can you seek out experiences of awe, such as staring at the stars, that will help to shift your perception?

5. RESOLVING CONFLICT

CREATING A PSYCHOLOGICALLY SAFE SPACE

We will always perform at our best in spaces where we feel psychologically safe. If an air of conflict hangs over us, we won't feel safe as we'll feel consistently vulnerable to 'attack'. Working in a tense environment is not conducive to an enjoyable experience or a space in which we can flourish.

Psychological safety in the workplace has been defined as "the belief that one will not be punished or humiliated for speaking up with ideas, questions, concerns, or mistakes, and that the team is safe for interpersonal risk taking."[17]

We want to feel empowered to take risks and give our opinions because this is how new, brilliant ideas come into play. There is always room for improvements to be made in the workplace, but the only way those will happen is if we are encouraged to give honest feedback and then work up a solution to enact the change. This could be anything from an internal improvement that will affect the workforce to a brilliant idea that will help customers.

COMING TO A RESOLUTION

It is not always possible to resolve conflict, but you owe it to yourself to try. If you are the junior person in the situation, the hope is that the more senior member of staff will instigate communication or offer an apology. However, as we all know, this doesn't always happen. Sometimes people are too proud or too unaware to know they have caused any issues.

If you are approached with an apology or an offer to discuss a conflict, your best course of action is to be open and to enter willingly into the process of reconciliation. There is always the option to make the approach yourself, even if you feel you're in the right.

Every conflict will require its own format for resolution, but a key requisite is to actively listen. Don't enter into the situation with your points ready to go and get so caught up with stating your case that you don't hear what the other person is saying. In order for a conclusion to be reached, there is likely to be compromise, which will involve negotiation of some sort. This will mean having to listen to the other party's issues so that you know what they want and how you can navigate towards a solution that works for you both. The best approach is to stay as calm as possible. Once elevated emotions enter into the equation, it's much harder to find common ground with the other person.

DEALING WITH DIFFICULT PEOPLE

If you need further resources, there is a brilliant and concise book called *Dealing with Difficult People*, published by Harvard Business Review Press, that gives a plethora of suggestions as to how to resolve conflict.[18]

PART FOUR NOTES

HANDLING REJECTION

MY TRIGGERS

NOT MAKING IT PERSONAL

HOW TO KEEP PERSPECTIVE

IDEAS FOR RESOLVING CONFLICT

"

We need emotional, physical and mental boundaries to protect us.

"

PART FIVE

BOUNDARY
SETTING

1. INTERFERENCE

It goes without saying that we are constantly contactable – at any time of the day and in several different ways. Phone calls, messages, social media, emails... no wonder we want to keep our phones on silent all the time, or we would be incessantly pinging.

The pings and vibrations are like a small child tugging at your sleeve for your attention. Every time one goes off, it's your phone asking you to give it a look. It doesn't care what you're doing at the time – it wants your attention, now. And then again in a few minutes' time. If you were to compare your phone to a colleague, how annoyed would you become with the amount of attention they were demanding from you, all the time, no matter what you were in the middle of?

EXTERNAL INTERRUPTIONS

External interruptions, whether work or home related, are a massive distraction from the tasks we have to do. And here's the killer statistic: it takes on average 23 minutes and 15 seconds to get back to the task you were originally doing.[19] This means you only have to be disrupted twice in an hour to be permanently distracted and get nothing done. Not only that, you will be working in a state of higher stress as you will be trying to work faster to compensate for the lack of time.

The answer? Put your phone on focus mode by turning off sounds and previews of your notifications. Block out an hour in your diary of protected time each day to get the work done that you need to do, and tell your colleagues that you won't be contactable during that time.

INTERNAL INTERRUPTIONS

The voices in our heads can be as powerful interruptions as the never-ending pings on our devices. And these ones are harder to turn off.

Our internal critical voices can be pretty loud and abusive. They don't have any boundaries and the fact is that they live inside us, so we can't tell them to leave. The way to keep these voices preoccupied will depend on the type of relationship you have with yours. How can you aim to maintain internal calm while you are trying to work? For example:

- Do your internal voices simply need recognition?
- Do they need appeasing?
- Can you write out a list of things that 'need to be done' sometime in the future so that the voices are no longer in your head and you can focus on the task at hand?

Remember that your brain is a tool. You control it, not the other way around.

2. OVERWORKING

PROTECTING YOURSELF FROM BURNOUT

When we're happy at work we aim to give our best, and our home lives deserve the same amount of input and attention. If we don't keep a check on ourselves, we could damage our relationships and work to the point of burnout.

If we are consistently prioritizing our work over the people we live with – our friends, family or partner – we are relegating them to second best position. It's quite obvious that this isn't going to feel great. They will start to feel rejected and may feel they have to compete for our time. After a while, they might just give up trying.

Being constantly available is not healthy when it comes to work. Many get trapped in the idea that being ever available makes them a gold-star employee. But it doesn't. Work quality slips and stress increases. You need your rest to recover your body and brain, which ultimately will make you a better employee.

WORKING, AND LIVING, FROM HOME

Challenges arise when our work and home lives blend into one and there is no clear distinction between the two. This has become more and more common thanks to the number of us who now work from home.

In February 2022, the UK's Office of National Statistics reported that "84% of workers who had to work from home because of the coronavirus pandemic said they planned to carry out a mix of working at home and in their place of work in the future."[20]

To separate your work and home lives, you need to clearly communicate your availability. If you need the physical separation, can you find a co-working space or a spot in your home to designate as your workspace? What signals can you use to clearly tell your family or others in your home that you're working and not to be disrupted? And then, can you put your out-of-office message on in the evenings to be clear that you won't respond until the next day, and give your home life the attention that you have just given your work?

Find your own way to protect your time and space.

THE BENEFITS OF BREAKS

Your brain will subconsciously work away on a problem that you set yourself no matter whether you are officially in work hours or not. Breaks allow you to physically rest and recover, but they also allow your brain to silently pick away at a problem while you are doing other things. Then, when it has arrived at a good conclusion, the thought will come to you while you are walking, taking a bath or on the loo.

3. ENERGY VAMPIRES

PROTECTING YOUR ENERGY

Energy vampires are devices, or most commonly people, that drain your energy dry. The clever thing about them is that you don't notice it happening until you have come away from them feeling exhausted and you aren't quite sure what happened.

Just like the vampires in the stories, energy vampires suck your energy away but slowly enough so that you don't see it happening. They need your energy in order to survive. They'll come away from your interaction feeling revived. You, however, will not. You might feel tired, perhaps even sick. When you look back at the interaction, you may realize that you've offered to help them – perhaps quite literally offering to do a task for them – or emotionally supported them in some way.

Highly sensitive people are commonly the prey of the energy vampire. In the same way that opposites attract, the energy vampire needs people who are eager to please and who want to 'fix' everything – in other words, people who will be their willing victims.

Judith Orloff's *The Empath's Survival Guide* is a great book for learning how to identify these people and objects and what to do about them.[21]

HOW TO PROTECT YOURSELF

In short, here are some key steps you can take to help yourself:

1. **Recognition is the first step.**
   How do you feel after an encounter?
   Feeling physically drained is the first sign.

2. **Don't pander to them.**
   Before you offer any support, stop yourself.
   Without you offering your help, they are likely to stop coming to you because you won't be giving them what they need.

3. **You can say no.**
   You have the power to say that you can't or don't want to do anything that is asked of you.

4. **Spend as little time with them as possible.**
   Remove yourself from their sphere of influence as much as you're able. If it's a colleague, stop your social interactions or add another willing person to the mix so there is an energetic buffer.

5. **Stick only to work conversations and avoid emotion if you can.**
   Stop taking on their emotional baggage and stick to the work at hand.

COLLEAGUES VS. FRIENDS

Being close to your co-workers is great. It creates bonds and trust, and generally makes your work life more enjoyable. It is to be encouraged given that we spend so much of our lives at work. But, as with any relationship, determine the type of person they are first. If they are an energy vampire, you have to be wary of the fact that you will be in constant contact, which is potentially eight hours a day when they could be 'taking' from you.

While it is not impossible, it is much harder to step back from a friendship than to lean into one.

THOUGHTS AND RESOLUTIONS

4. EMOTIONAL DUMPING

THE UNPROFESSIONAL ART OF OVERSHARING

"Emotional Dumping, also known as Trauma Dumping or Toxic Venting, is the act of unconsciously expressing feelings without the awareness and consideration of the other person's emotional state."
(Online Counselling Service[22])

EMOTIONAL DUMPING VS. SHARING EXPERIENCES

There are some key differences between emotional dumping and sharing experiences – so you don't have to worry that every time you want to talk about a problem with a friend, you are negatively impinging on their life. It is, after all, important to share our issues with friends to get their perspective and support.

Emotional dumping looks something like this:

- The other person's issues are coming at you thick and fast, and you have not been given a way out. It's quite overwhelming.
- They are talking about issues that may also have affected you but there is no consideration for any of your potential past traumas connected to the topic.
- There is no consideration for your time.
- It feels like a one-way conversation (which, in fact, is not a conversation at all but a monologue).
- They are looking to blame you or others and want your support.
- You walk away feeling as though you've taken on their issues somehow and are worse off for it.

This is not the same as sharing experiences and asking for support, where the person explains the issues they have, asks for advice, listens and is comforted.

THE KEY? ASK PERMISSION TO VENT AND SHARE

To avoid emotionally dumping on others, first check:

- What state of mind they are in
- Whether talking through your issues will trigger any of their own problems
- Whether they have time for you

This can be a quick as, "I'm having a rough day at work with X. Do you have ten minutes for us to chat so that I can get your opinion?" Don't be upset if the other person says no – just like you on some days, they might not have the capacity to help you at that moment in the way that they'd like.

SHARING PROFESSIONALLY

Oversharing could look like one person dominating a four-person meeting by taking five minutes to tell the others about their weekend. The likelihood is that the other participants don't really care that much – they want to get on with the meeting so they don't end up having to work late. Check yourself if this is you. Giving short answers to social questions is respectful of everyone's time. And if the content of your anecdote seems a touch inappropriate, then it probably is.

THOUGHTS AND RESOLUTIONS

5. WORK DUMPING

BEING DUMPED ON

When you're the newbie, it's easy to be keen and to say yes to everything. Being keen is great. We don't want to discourage this type of behaviour. Saying 'yes' to everything, however, can lead to taking on way too much. If you take on too much, you won't have time to do it all – let alone do a good job of it – and your work quality may plummet, despite your best intentions. It's important to get a grip quite quickly on what you can manage and what you can't.

Be wary of the 'dumpers', too. There are always a few lurking around any organization. These are the opportunists who look out for keen beans and use that enthusiasm as an open door to hand over their workload in the name of 'development' and 'providing a great opportunity'. Once you've clocked who these people are, you will need to learn how to say no. Share this information with your line manager as you can use them as a means of protection. A suitable response might be, "Let me check with my manager before I take this on."

HOW TO PROTECT YOURSELF

It may be that the dumper is your line manager! If so, here are some things you can do:

- **Say no but be sure to explain why.** You are allowed to say no, but only with a valid reason. Explain how long similar work took you before, the time you need to set aside and the knock-on effect that the new work would have on other projects. Be transparent about what's on your plate.

- **Ask for their help to prioritize.** Ask your line manager what you should start with and prioritize. With them on board, and in full view of your to-do list, they have become a part of the decision-making process.

- **Ask for support.** You may not feel equipped to take on the task just yet. If so, ask for relevant training or expertise from another person so that you can learn how to do the task. Once you have had that support, you can consider yourself set to take on the same task in the future, but on your own.

STEP OUT OF YOUR COMFORT ZONE

Don't get caught in the trap of saying no to something because it scares you. A necessary part of progression is taking on work that sits outside your comfort zone. In fact, doing things that we aren't originally comfortable with can be our biggest confidence boosters. Once we've successfully tackled the new thing, we've adopted a new skill and have created a positively reinforcing confidence loop that means we'll try new things again. And don't worry if it goes wrong – we'll be dealing with that in *Part Eight*.

PART FIVE NOTES

PREVENTING INTERFERENCE

AVOID OVERWORKING

DEALING WITH ENERGY VAMPIRES

PROTECTING MYSELF FROM EMOTIONAL DUMPING

PROTECTING MYSELF FROM WORK DUMPING

"

Positive validation keeps us in motion.

"

PART SIX

FINDING YOUR STRIDE

1. ENTHUSIASM CYCLES

HOW TO MAKE THEM WORK FOR YOU

Part Three looked at ways to predict our energy cycles on both a personal level and a bigger-picture level. This foresight means that we can plan and capitalize on our time based on how we think we will feel.

It's great when we're riding the highs. We have the energy to be resilient, which means it's harder to knock us back even if things do go wrong. We feel capable and confident. As I'm sure you've experienced, it's much harder to work through low energy cycles. When we're feeling run-down, overwhelmed, stressed... you name it... it's much harder to find the gusto to tackle big problems, and it becomes much more of a struggle to get up when we've been knocked down.

WHEN YOU'RE LOW, FAKE POSITIVITY

A low-mood loop is a cycle in which, because we feel rubbish and have negative thoughts, we stop exercising, sleeping properly and eating so well. We start to put less effort into ourselves. Because we are then denying ourselves proper nourishment, exercise and a proper night's sleep, we are taking away three vital factors that help to keep us in a positive state of mind. Keeping an eye on these three factors is your first step to good mental health.

So how can you dig yourself out of a low-mood loop when you find yourself in it? You need to fake it until you start to feel better again. You need to take yourself out for exercise, eat well and try to get the best sleep you can (easier said than done). You need to fake positivity until it works. Dr Julie Smith's book *Why Has Nobody Told Me This Before?* is a great one to read if you want to explore this idea further.[23]

It's been proven that by faking a smile, we make ourselves happier, so you can always start there: "When you forcefully practise smiling, it stimulates the amygdala – the emotional centre of the brain – which releases neurotransmitters to encourage an emotionally positive state," says research from the University of South Australia.[24]

WHEN YOU'RE HIGH, CAPITALIZE

On the flipside, when you're riding the crest of that wave and you have excess energy, what tasks can you take on that will help future you? Author Kevin Duncan calls this 'precrastination': using your time to think about problems that are likely to arise.[25] Future you will be grateful that past you was so considerate.

THOUGHTS AND RESOLUTIONS

2. RECOGNIZING YOUR GOOD BITS

GETTING INTO YOUR FLOW

Positive validation keeps us in motion. It's what motivates us to continue and reinforces our behaviours. There are two major components to feeling validated. The first is receiving external recognition, with others praising your work and telling you how well you're doing. The second is an internal sense of contentment, where we know what we love doing and are good at doing it. We want a balance of both in our work lives. You need to be doing a good job that is recognized externally by others, but you also want to enjoy what you're doing, so you get your own sense of satisfaction.

GETTING INTO FLOW AND INTERNAL SATISFACTION

Flow is a state of mind. When you're in it, you don't notice the time that goes by. Mihaly Csikszentmihalyi wrote a book called *Flow* that explores this idea in detail.[26] Essentially, when in flow, you are so enraptured with the task at hand that the rest of the world falls away, and the task becomes meditative in its own right. You can find your flow in so many things – exercise, cooking, dancing, writing… experiment and see what works for you.

Flow has been shown to make people 500% more productive and more creative. It can also cut our learning times in half. While it lasts, we forget all the unpleasant aspects of life. We feel utterly content, in control, and aligned inside and out.

When we're in flow, five of our most powerful feelgood chemicals start to surge: dopamine (a reward chemical), norepinephrine (which drives focus and excitement), anandamide (which relieves pain), endorphins (the body's own natural high) and serotonin (which gives a calming effect).

What gets you into a flow state? Can you bring this into your work life? If you love what you are doing, you will do it more and will become better at it. So there is a natural progression in the sense that doing what you love means you'll – hopefully – be doing a great job.

RECEIVING PRAISE AND EXTERNAL VALIDATION

We like being told that we're good at what we're doing. Compliments encourage more of that behaviour as we ultimately want to be accepted by our group. If we want to do a good job, we'll aim to do the same behaviour again and again to prove our worth.

Take note of what you're being complimented on – it might be how you tackled a difficult situation or that you are the highest-billing salesperson in a month. By keeping track of how you did these praiseworthy tasks, you can rinse and repeat the same processes again for further brownie points. You should also document these metaphorical gold stars so you can bring them up at your next review to help towards a potential promotion.

It's important, however, not to solely focus on the praise you're receiving. You might be told you're doing a great job when doing something that you don't enjoy. The risk is that you therefore keep doing the job that you don't like because you have been praised for it. But you don't want to be stuck in a cycle of only doing the jobs with which you're not enamoured. Just because you are great at making a cup of tea for a colleague doesn't mean you want to always be the one making tea! So, beyond the praise, there must be a sense that your work aligns with your interests.

THOUGHTS AND RESOLUTIONS

3. WORKING ON THE BAD BITS

HOW TO CONQUER OUR WEAKNESSES AND DEVELOP AS A PERSON

While it might sound appealing, we can't avoid doing all the things that we're bad at. We tend to procrastinate when it comes to the jobs we don't love – putting them to the side for as long as we can and allowing them to loom over us. But it's these exact things that we need to tackle head on, as soon as they arrive. We don't need any dark clouds hovering around for extended periods of time. It's also often these tasks that most highlight to us potential areas for growth.

ASK YOUR AVOIDANT SELF
The first question to ask is: Why do you not want to do it? Sometimes the things we don't want to do are the things we need to do the most.

On a practical level, the desire to avoid a task may reveal gaps in your learning that need to be filled. If this is the case, what can you learn to acquire this knowledge? You may find that, once you know how to do it, it's not a scary task and that you enjoy yourself.

On an emotional level, the desire to avoid a task may reveal avoidant patterns within yourself. For example, you might not attempt something because there is a risk that you'll fail, and you don't want to feel the dissatisfaction that comes with not succeeding. The root of this is a fear of failure that prevents you from getting on with what you need to do – and you can't afford to get stuck in a loop where you don't do things for fear of an outcome, or you will never move forward.

GETTING ON WITH IT

If it's an essential part of the job, you simply have to get on with it. Not all of us love unblocking the drain, but we know we have to do it. (But if you do find that you love unblocking drains, perhaps becoming a plumber is the way forward for you.) It's nearly impossible to set up a work situation where you love 100% of what you do, every day.

The trick is to do any unfavoured jobs enough times that you accept them and can do them well, so that you can carry them out as quickly and painlessly as possible.

THE ART OF DELEGATION

Remember that you can always delegate – down to your juniors, upwards to your managers and sideways to your colleagues. It's likely there will be someone out there who *does* enjoy the job that you don't.

But before you delegate, attempt the task yourself. You should try everything once. If you still don't like it and it's not essential for you to do it, then you don't have to do it again. But at least you will be able to talk from a place of authority and empathy when someone else takes it on.

4. COMMUNICATING HOW YOU WORK BEST

HOW TO WORK WELL WITH YOUR TEAM

WHO IS DOING WHAT?

An obvious (but often overlooked) question is – do you know what your role is? How does it differ to your colleagues? Having clear task definition is important so you don't step on each other's toes. This will stem any battle of egos or an unhealthy sense of competition.

STAVE OFF MICROMANAGEMENT

Being micromanaged can be incredibly annoying. You don't feel trusted by your manager to get on with the job, and you are also incessantly interrupted (which, as *Part Five* outlined, can be hugely wasteful of your time). If this starts to happen, agree with your manager about how best to update them on your tasks. Would a daily ten-minute catch-up be best, or a weekly email listing what you've achieved and found challenging?

VOCALIZE YOUR LIKES

It's helpful for a manager to know what you like doing and what you don't. Most well-intentioned managers will want to know what you like doing and to see you excel at it. It looks good for them if you do well. But you have to be willing to give everything a go. You must also be prepared to do the things that you don't love doing.

SPEAK UP IF THERE IS A PROBLEM

When you come across a problem, do not hide it away and hope that it will disappear. It won't. The longer you leave it, the bigger it will get. It will be harder to sort out, and will hang uncomfortably over your head. As soon as you come across an issue, share it with your line manager or relevant colleague. Whether it's your fault or not, you need someone to help you get through this and help relieve the pressure. Your manager will come to trust you if they know that you will share any issues with them. These moments can also be a great chance to become the problem solver – a highly valued trait in any employee.

KEEP EVERYONE IN THE LOOP

The more knowledge they have, the more comfortable managers and the wider team will feel. When you get the chance, explain what you have on your to-do list, your priorities and your challenges. It'll be recognized that you're getting on with stuff and can be trusted, and this should help to give you the space that you need to get on with your job.

5. A HEALTHY ATTITUDE

REALISM VS. OPTIMISM

Being either relentlessly optimistic or unwaveringly pessimistic doesn't tend to work well. Here's why.

PESSIMISTS CAN BE BLOCKERS

Pessimists focus on the negative and default to cynicism, which is a non-starter. These are the people who say, "Here's why you can't do this" or "This is a bad idea because..." With enough negativity, anyone can be discouraged from taking on a project. You will talk yourself out of it before you even begin and actively discourage others from wanting to get involved. The way to get around this is to make sure you're suggesting solutions if you're the one highlighting the problem.

THE OPTIMISM TRAP

Optimists are great to be around because they usually look through rose-tinted glasses and assume the best possible outcome. And, most of the time, this comes with a sense of keenness and eagerness to please. The trap for optimists is that they may assume a positive result without digging into the detail and analysing whether something will actually work or not. Very often they will over-promise and things won't work out. The optimist will look as though they've failed, and faith in them may wear away, despite their best intentions.

OPTIMISTIC REALISM

So, what's the balance? Ideally, we want a positive outlook, but we need to make sure we aren't ignoring the reality of the situation.

A healthy balance is optimistic realism. Have a positive attitude, but before saying yes or embarking on anything, check its feasibility first. It's always okay to say, "This sounds like a great idea – let me look into the feasibility of it and get back to you before committing to anything." If it's not going to work, find another way. This is how you become a highly trusted employee. You become a pleasure to work with while constantly troubleshooting problems and working out ways to solve them.

"

When you're high, capitalize.

"

PART SIX NOTES

IDEAS FOR SUSTAINING ENTHUSIASM

MY GOOD BITS

MY BAD BITS

COMMUNICATING HOW I WORK BEST

HOW TO KEEP A HEALTHY ATTITUDE

"

It's your job to package up your achievements and to present them to the powers that be.

"

HOW TO GET PROMOTED

1. MEASURE YOUR PROGRESS

ASK FOR AND ANALYSE PERFORMANCE INDICATORS, AND STICK TO THEM

There will come a point when you are ready for a promotion. With it usually comes higher status, higher pay and recognition that you are doing a good job.

> "Male employees are twice as likely to ask for a pay rise in comparison to female colleagues."
> (Censuswide survey, April 2021[27])

DISCUSS THE PROMOTION

Put your hand up for a promotion, whether the role that you'd be promoted to exists or not. Think about what it is that you want. Do you want more money but are happy with the same job title? Or vice versa – are you happy with the pay but want a jump in status? Usually they come hand in hand, but it's good to have evaluated what's important to you and why.

Ask your line manager to be honest about timelines and whether there is a real possibility of a promotion coming to fruition. If there are no opportunities for a promotion in the organization, this might be where you start to look at other options. But at least you've given your manager the chance to try and keep you, and you have been transparent about what you want.

Take a look at what your desired role requires. Compare this to the job that you are currently doing. You may find that you are already doing a lot of the things that would be required of you if you moved up a level. If this is the case, you can already start to compile a case to prove your competencies.

MAKE A PLAN

The next step is to co-create a plan with your line manager to get you to the next level. You need to create set objectives – some call these key performance indicators (or KPIs) – that you can work towards achieving. Make sure:

- They are measurable so you can prove when you have accomplished them
- You have direct control over them and you're not relying on others' input
- They demonstrate to the organization that you are capable
- There aren't so many that it will be impossible to achieve them all
- You schedule a review with your manager after a set period, such as six months, so that the KPIs aren't forgotten

ALIGN WITH THE ORGANIZATION

Take a look at the question of your potential promotion from the organization's point of view. You will have a much higher chance of success if you are both pulling in the same direction and if you are helping the organization to achieve its own targets. It also shows that you are thinking like a leader if you articulate that you have been considering the matter from both a personal viewpoint and an organizational perspective.

What are the organization's overarching strategy and goals?
How can you take the organization's targets and values and input them into your own objectives?

THOUGHTS AND RESOLUTIONS

2. BE KEEN

PUT YOUR HAND UP FOR THINGS

In one survey, 62% of employers said that having a negative or pessimistic attitude hurt an employee's chance for promotion.[28]

BE WILLING AND ABLE

Putting your hand up for things, extracurricular or not, is a surefire way to stand out among your peers. It shows an eagerness to help, a desire to support your team and an interest in the projects being put forward to you.

Think of it this way. As a manager, if you had three direct reports and the chance to promote one of them, would you pick the individual who was always offering to help and seemed keen, or those who sat back in their chairs and kept themselves quiet?

SEE IT AS AN OPPORTUNITY TO LEARN

Any projects that you take on outside your usual scope of work will be great chances to learn something new, meet other people in the organization, and get in front of others who might have a way in when it comes to your promotion.

If you end up working with other departments, you'll gain an understanding of how the company works from a more holistic perspective. It will give you first-hand experience of other areas of the organization that you may get the opportunity to move across to, should that seem appealing. You might prefer what they do or the people you'd be working with, or they might be the department that is offering a promotion when yours isn't.

PROACTIVE PROBLEM SOLVING

Even better than putting your hand up in *reaction* to projects coming your way – can you be *proactive*? Being proactive shows great initiative as well as leader-like qualities. When you're the boss, you won't be told what to do every day – at this level you'll have to notice what needs to be done and delegate to others.

Once you've settled in, it is highly likely that you'll find some areas that could use some improvement. There may be a process that is clunky, a report that needs to be made more interesting or a cultural change that needs to take place. No organization is perfect so there are always things that can be updated. Very often it's only those who work with these everyday protocols – the more junior members of staff – who spot such issues. The bosses are busy fighting more dramatic fires so it's unlikely that these everyday improvements will be high on their agenda.

Problem solving is one of the key attributes you need to be a leader. Therefore, by proactively finding a solution, you are already demonstrating the skills you need to lead.

If you find one of these issues, what could you, or a team of people you gather together, do to help improve it?

THOUGHTS AND RESOLUTIONS

3. BE SEEN

MEET OTHER TEAM MEMBERS AND INDUSTRY FOLK

NETWORKING

Most of us recoil at the word 'networking.' But, when done well, it can be an incredibly powerful tool, and it does not have to involve awkwardly standing around at an industry event trying to elbow your way into a conversation with new people.

Firstly, find people of interest in the organization that you'd like to talk to. Maybe they achieved something great. Maybe you're interested in how they got to where they are. Perhaps you're really intrigued by their job and want to know more. When you find these people, ask for 30 minutes of their time. They will (most likely) be flattered by the request and it will put you on their radar. It never hurts to have people higher up know your name.

When it comes to getting promotions, there is usually a signing-off process where board members approve your upward move. If this is the case, it's incredibly helpful if they have heard of you and therefore can vouch for you.

You don't have to limit your efforts to people in your organization – look to the wider industry and others that inspire you.

PRESENT YOURSELF WELL

> In one survey, 27% of employers said that having attire too casual for the workplace could affect employees' chance of a promotion.[29]

Controversial or not, it's important to be aware of the fact that what you wear can affect your chances of moving up the ranks. It reflects your attitudes and awareness of the space you're about to enter. What I wear for a wedding will be different from what I wear to meet friends. It is more than a way of expressing ourselves – it's a way of showing respect for the social situation we find ourselves in.

The same goes with work clothes. Gone are the days when suits were the only acceptable attire and women had to wear heels to show status, thankfully. But we should be wary of taking it too far the other way. What would wearing a tracksuit say in your place of work? At a leisurewear company, that might be the done thing. If you're working as an estate agent, perhaps less so.

Expressing individuality and creativity through clothes should be applauded, but we should show self-awareness when it comes to what is and isn't appropriate in the workplace. It shows that you are capable of reading your surroundings – which is a vital attribute in business.

If you're not 100% sure, swap the flip-flops for something else. If you think it might come across as too casual, get a second opinion from a friend or colleague who you know will tell you straight.

THOUGHTS AND RESOLUTIONS

4. BE HEARD

FRAME YOUR ACHIEVEMENTS
AND TALK ABOUT THEM

So, you're keen, you're visible and you want to be heard. You want your voice to carry weight and your opinions to be respected. For some people, speaking up is no problem at all. For others, the idea feels hugely uncomfortable.

INTROVERTS

The more introverted of us need to find ways to step into our power and make sure our voices are heard, because they are just as important as the others in the room. If you're in a meeting, try saying something in the first few minutes. It will make it far less daunting when you next have the inclination to speak up. Keep in mind that it's not how much you say but the quality that counts. Concise and thoughtful reflections are far more powerful than a never-ending torrent of words that fill up airtime.

EXTRAVERTS

For the extraverts, don't speak for the sake of it just to fill up space. It can be a bit like crying wolf – if colleagues expect what you say to have no substance, they'll stop listening to you. Another trap is to project your own thoughts while not listening to what's being said. Make sure that you are actively listening to the direction of the meeting and are responding to it. The others in the meeting will disengage with you if they don't feel like they're being heard or you are completely off topic.

FRAMING YOUR ACHIEVEMENTS

Beyond being heard in the day-to-day, you want to make sure your achievements are recognized. You can be your own best advocate in these instances. It's your job to package up what you've achieved and present it to the powers that be.

How have you made an impact?
- Are there particular projects that you worked on that have done really well?
- Have you come up with any pioneering ideas or ways of working?
- Did you find a problem and proactively solve it?
- Did you handle a tricky situation especially well?
- Have you brought in new customers to the business?

Keep track of all the minor and major activities that you've been a part of and record them. It will be very useful to be able to present these to your manager when you're chatting about your promotion. Ideally, they will be undeniable ways in which you have helped.

5. STAND OUT

SELF-PROMOTION

At the beginning of your career, it is your responsibility to advocate for yourself. To stand above the rest, you need to be visible. So the question is: What can you do to publicize yourself and become recognized by your industry?

- Could you write an article for an industry blog or publication?
- Could you put yourself forward for panel discussions on certain topics that you feel comfortable with?
- What events could you put yourself forward to talk at?

AWARDS

Search and ask around to see if your industry has any awards that recognize excellent work. It's highly likely that it does. Take a look at the categories and pick out a few that might work for you. You could enter as an individual or as a team, or put forward a project that you worked on that generated great results. Winning awards is great for everyone – the client or customer, you, the organization and the team. No one can argue with your achievements if an external body has given you a gold stamp of brilliance.

I know from experience how powerful winning awards can be – this was one of the biggest factors that led me to promotions and job hires, and is still something I use to this day. Once you've won an award, no one can take it away from you.

BECOME THE GO-TO EXPERT

You know you're onto something when you become the go-to person for certain topics. You are becoming a valuable member of an organization, known for your expertise. This is a fantastic position to be in and one for which you should strive. Is there a topic that you could strive to be an expert on?

"

It's not how much you say but the quality that counts.

"

PART SEVEN NOTES

WHAT TO MEASURE

HOW CAN I BE KEEN?

HOW CAN I BE SEEN?

HOW CAN I BE HEARD?

HOW CAN I STAND OUT?

"

It is an absolute guarantee that, at some point, you will mess up.

"

WHEN THINGS
GET TOUGH

1. WHAT TO DO WHEN YOU SCREW UP

HOW TO HANDLE YOUR MISTAKES

It is an absolute guarantee that, at some point, you will mess up. You might make a mistake in a spreadsheet that skews your business figures or you might leave your laptop on a train. Rest assured that something like this will happen – it's an inevitable part of operations, especially when you're new to something. Take solace in the knowledge that everyone does it at some point.

WHY YOU NEED TO FESS UP

Assess the situation and see if there is anything immediate that you can do to rectify it. Then, whether the situation is rectified or not, tell your line manager straight away. If you have solved the issue, then you are showing the valuable trait of being able to spot mistakes and self-correct. And if you haven't, you'll need a hand.

Transparency and humility are your best friends right now. Hiding an issue in the hope that it will go away is dangerous. These things don't just disappear – they silently snowball until they dramatically rear their ugly heads, potentially taking you down with them.

Even though it may seem counterintuitive, by sharing the issue and admitting your mistakes, you show that you are trustworthy and know when to engage the higher powers to help.

ASK FOR HELP

Even better than dealing appropriately with a mistake is predicting when you will make one. If you have an ungainly spreadsheet to fill out, ask if a teammate can check your work before it becomes public. If you are struggling with something and aren't 100% sure what you're doing (which arguably is a lot of us a lot of the time), then go and ask someone who does. If you've been sent a nasty email that you have to respond to, confer with your manager before replying. If they're a good manager, they might even take matters into their own hands and protect you if the criticism is unfounded.

REPEAT OFFENDERS

Try as hard as you can not to make the same mistake more than once. Twice is forgivable, but three times starts to look like negligence. The key factor here will be your attitude towards the situation. If you are persistently trying, taking your time to get it right and engaging help, but it's still not working, then you have grounds to ask for a different task or a workaround. If, however, it looks like you've given up because you don't care any more, it could start to look like an attitude and competency issue. You should aim to avoid this because it is not a great foundation for getting that promotion you've been asking for.

2. BULLYING

IDENTIFYING THEM

> "Workplace bullying is harmful, targeted behavior that happens at work. It might be spiteful, offensive, mocking, or intimidating. It forms a pattern, and it tends to be directed at one person or a few people."
> (Crystal Raypole, Healthline[30])

Being bullied is no fun. I have been a victim of it myself and I know how it can affect your work quality, home life, self-confidence and levels of anxiety. In my case, my boss was taking out anger on me that should have been directed elsewhere, but it was me who got shouted at until I cried, with everyone in the office watching, while he made unfounded statements. This happened at least once a week. I had to quit that job in the end because of the negative effects it was having on my mental health, which impacted my day-to-day personal life. And it carried with me even after that job. I was so used to being battered down that I was afraid to speak up, even in new, 'safe' jobs.

In my instance, I reported the person to human resources and then I quit. This is just one way of dealing with bullying – and a rather extreme way at that. There will be codes of conduct in place to help deal with bullying situations. The first thing to do is to approach your human resources team, safe in the knowledge that they are obligated to keep your conversations confidential unless you request otherwise.

UNEMOTIONAL CRITICISM ISN'T BULLYING – BUT...

Remember that if you are being fairly criticized, then this is not bullying. An important part of your manager's role is to guide and teach you – which will include pointing out where you could do things better. Without this feedback, your development will suffer. But if you are constantly being put down and made to feel worthless, that's different.

Feedback without emotion is helpful guidance, whereas feedback loaded with misdirected emotional baggage will make you feel like crap. There are so many forms that this can take. Start by asking these two questions:
- How is it making you feel?
- Can you see injustice in how you are being treated?

CHECK YOUR OWN BEHAVIOUR

One of the best things we can do is analyse our own behaviour. Make it a steadfast rule that you won't take your anger out on other people. Let others know if you're having a bad day or are incredibly busy – and that that's why your answers may come across differently. Don't become the bully yourself.

THOUGHTS AND RESOLUTIONS

3. FEELING OVERWHELMED

THE USUAL SUSPECTS AND HOW TO TACKLE THEM

It's usual to feel that there is a lot to take in when you start a new job. There will be a lot of new information, new people and new systems to get to grips with.

TIME ANXIETY

Time anxiety is the feeling that you never have enough time in your day to accomplish your to-do list. Now that we work in a world where we are constantly contactable at any time of day, are often expected to be 'always on' and commonly have several screens on the go, there is no end to the incoming requests. Combine a forever-full inbox with an eagerness to please your new employer and you have yourself a potential dilemma.

Take notice if you are waking up worrying about getting everything done. Acknowledge that multitasking is not a viable way to do a great job*. Then look at your to-do list and prioritize. If you are worrying, let your manager know. Let them help you to determine how best to manage your time so that you do a good job and don't feel engulfed by it all.

PRODUCTIVITY SHAME

Productivity shame comes in two forms:

- The idea that however much you do, it isn't enough
- The feeling that you aren't allowed to relax and be 'unproductive'

Nowadays, society commonly measures us by our productivity. We gloat about what we have achieved and created and (perhaps sadly) aren't encouraged to brag about how much time we've spent on the sofa. I myself am a glutton for showing how much I've achieved based on my outputs, and in the past this was how I validated my successes. But what I didn't realize was that I was running myself into the ground for an audience who didn't necessarily care about the amount I was producing.

We all need to learn the very real benefits of rest and recovery and doing nothing. It doesn't just make life a more pleasurable experience but also makes us better at what we do when we are in our productive phases (*Part Three* and *Part Six* have more on this topic).

THOUGHTS AND RESOLUTIONS

---

* "Why you can't multitask"
https://www.psychologytoday.com/gb/blog creative-leadership/201811/
why-you-cant-multi-task

4. WHEN LIFE GETS IN THE WAY

WHEN PERSONAL ISSUES GET ON TOP OF YOU

It is a sad but inevitable truth that at some point we will face challenging events in our lives – death, divorce, sickness or a global catastrophe, to name but a few. Unless you are adept at compartmentalizing, the truth is that our personal issues will affect our working lives.

WORK AS A DISTRACTION

In some cases, work can come as a welcome distraction from the all-consuming thoughts that surround negative situations. It might be harder to concentrate on work, and you may feel less motivated to sit down and do it, but working can act as a short-term preoccupation. It is something that you have control over – potentially unlike the unfolding drama surrounding you. Having a space where you can be respected and praised for your competence may be very helpful to keep you afloat through tough times.

In an ideal world, work wouldn't be used as a means to avoid facing your personal issues completely. In the same way that burying a problem in the hope that it will go away is not a good idea, ignoring your personal issues through avoidance will also not solve the problem. Your issues will sit there and wait for you to face them whether you like it or not.

YOU CONTROL THE NARRATIVE

At work you are the filter for your narrative. You are in charge of what you do – and don't – tell your colleagues. While your own world may be slipping away around you, you have agency over the story you present.

You may want to keep your issues to yourself as work is a space in which you can live a 'normal' life unfettered by questions and pity. Alternatively, you may want to be very open about what's happening so that your colleagues are aware and can be considerate with you. Most colleagues will prefer not to upset you if they have the choice and are aware of your situation.

I would recommend being transparent with your manager about what's happening. You may need some back up if you have to take some last-minute time off work or are feeling particularly sensitive. They can't be sympathetic, or help to support you, if they don't know what's going on.

THOUGHTS AND RESOLUTIONS

5. BEING HONEST WITH YOURSELF

MORE, LESS, OR JUST ABOUT RIGHT?

ARE YOU PUTTING IN EVERYTHING THAT YOU CAN?

It would be unrealistic to assume that everyone who ever entered the world of work was keen, eager to please, interested and willing to put their hand up for everything. The likelihood is that, if you are reading this book, you care about being good at what you do. But we are not all built like this all the time.

If we want to be recognized, praised and promoted, we need to be putting in the effort to deserve it. Give yourself a really honest answer to this question: Are you putting in everything that you can?

DO YOU FEEL LIKE A FRAUD?

"[Impostor syndrome is] the name given to a psychological pattern of thinking, characterised by persistent feelings of inadequacy, self-doubt and fears of being exposed as a fraud. Individuals who feel like impostors typically downplay their own achievements, think their successes in life are down to luck and chance, and have difficulty accepting compliments and praise."
(Isabelle Kirk, YouGov[31])

Even the most successful people suffer from impostor syndrome – the feeling that at some point they will be 'found out' and everyone will suddenly realize that they are frauds and don't know what they're doing. It is surprisingly common, with two thirds of Britons saying they have difficulty accepting compliments.[32]

To try and counter these feelings, it is common to work harder, create higher standards for yourself and put in exceptional effort. But this way of working is not always tenable in the long term. It can be exhausting and impossible to maintain, and your colleagues will start to expect 150% as an everyday output.

Do you have impostor syndrome? The first thing to do is to acknowledge these feelings of self-doubt. Interrogate why they are there. The likelihood is that these feelings originate from experiences that aren't related to the job you are doing now. Try to take the pressure off and treat yourself with compassion.

It will take time to get out of the habit of piling the pressure on yourself – but if a habit can be created, it can be undone. Stay aware of your self-talk, amend your rhetoric and be kind to yourself.

PART EIGHT NOTES

WHAT TO DO WHEN I SCREW UP

BULLYING

DEALING WITH OVERWHELM

WHAT TO DO WHEN LIFE GETS IN THE WAY

BEING HONEST WITH MYSELF

"

We all deserve
to be as happy
as we can for
as much as our
lives as possible.

"

STAYING
OR GOING?

1. YOUR JOY PERCENTAGE

HOW MUCH OF YOUR TIME ARE YOU ENJOYING?

"Joy is what makes life worth living... and yet for some reason we have decided it is superfluous – the icing on the cake, rather than an integral part of the cake itself."
(Ingrid Fetell Lee, *Joyful*[33])

WHAT IS YOUR JOY PERCENTAGE?

If you asked yourself how much of your time was spent in joy, I wonder what your answer would be. When I asked myself the same question a few years ago, my answer was around the 50% mark. About half of my time was spent doing things that made me feel happy and content. My conclusion was that half of my time was not enough. I should be striving to make that percentage as close to the 100% mark as possible. We all deserve to be as happy as we can for as much of our lives as possible.

WHAT IS JOY?

Joy can be cultivated regardless of your circumstances.

> "Joy and happiness are often used interchangeably.
> However, happiness technically refers to the pleasurable
> feelings (emotions) that result from a situation, experience,
> or objects, whereas joy is a state of mind that can be found
> even in times of grief or uncertainty. Thus, we can work on
> cultivating joy independent of our circumstances."
> (Stephanie Collier, Harvard Health Publishing[34])

Seeing joy as a state of mind is not a new concept. The Stoics,
who created a school of philosophy in ancient Greece and Rome
in the 3rd century BCE, saw joy as a "deep state of being" that
comes "from purpose, excellence and duty."[35]

FINDING JOY IN THE EVERYDAY

It's easy to miss the moments that we should savour when we're
busy worrying about the future or focusing on other issues. The
first step is to acknowledge whether, right now in this moment,
you are feeling unease or contentment. If it's the latter, fantastic.
If it's the former, what can you do to adjust the situation? Is it a
physical change that you need to make, or can you reframe your
circumstances to see the more positive side?

Reframing is an incredibly powerful tool. We can't always control what happens to us, but we can control how we react. By taking a circumstance and looking at it in a different light, you can adjust your attitude and therefore how you feel. You can turn negative occurrences into positive ones. By doing this, you are well on your way to living in a more joyful state.

THOUGHTS AND RESOLUTIONS

2. IS IT YOU OR IS IT THE JOB?

IS IT AN UNSETTLEDNESS WITHIN YOU, OR THE WORK?

"Around 70% of all working-age people are actively looking for a job change... For workers age 25 to 34, the median tenure is 3.2 years."[36]

ATTITUDES TO CAREER CHANGE

Gone are the days of lifelong careers. As someone who enjoys variety and learning new things, I see this as a good thing. It has, however, meant that the more recent generations have been dubbed as flaky and uncommitted by those brought up in the eras beforehand.

Particularly, a lot has changed in the past ten years. The BBC reports that "Gen Zers... are the cohort most likely to quit if they're unsatisfied at work."[37]

CHECK YOUR SITUATION

Before you throw in the towel at work, you need to have a think about *why* you want to do so. Very often our work is the easiest thing to change – much more so than uprooting where we live or who our partner is. Moving house or ending a relationship requires a lot of emotional exertion. Changing jobs can easily be explained to our friends, especially as we control the narrative, and is something we can keep at a distance – unlike issues at home.

The key question is: Are you unsettled because of the job, or is there another aspect of your life that may need to be addressed?

You may not love the answer. But unless you tackle what needs to be tackled, the unsettledness will remain no matter how many times you move job.

CREATE A TRIGGERS LIST

Come back to the trigger points that you analysed in *Part Four*. List what it is in your job that is bothering you. Perhaps it's an annoying person, a task that you don't like or a lack of satisfaction. This could be a perfect moment for some self-development. If it's a person that irritates you, try looking at the characteristics that irk you and determine whether you can adjust yourself to be more accommodating or understanding. After all, there is never a guarantee that another job won't deliver someone even more bothersome!

Look at yourself first, adapt what you can, learn more about who you are and then – if all is still not well – start to see what other opportunities are out there.

3. WHAT WOULD CHANGE?

IF YOU MOVE JOB,
WILL THE ISSUES BE THE SAME?

TOO MANY MOVES

Moving job too many times in the first decade of your working life can raise red flags for a potential employer. It may give the impression either that you are uncommitted and happy to jump ship as soon as another opportunity arises, or that you aren't great at your job and organizations are happy to let you go. Neither of these look good.

So it's always worth ensuring that you are 100% certain that you want to leave, that you have tried your best to make the situation work, and therefore that you have a true and convincing story to tell future employers about why it was your time to leave.

Also bear in mind that you only have one shot at threatening to leave. Once you have used that card, you can't use it again – you will be crying wolf and they won't take you seriously. So make sure you use it wisely. Unless there is something your employers can do to make you stay – such as raise your salary or promote you – you may decide there is no room for negotiation, and therefore there is no conversation to be had in the first place.

THE GRASS IS NOT ALWAYS GREENER

Needless to say, the grass is not always greener in a new job. Six months in, once the shininess has dimmed and you are expected to have got to grips with the way things work, you might end up with the same issues that you had previously. You should try to avoid this. You need to look at what it is that's making you unhappy and whether the new job will genuinely make things better.

WHAT NEEDS TO CHANGE

So, what are your pain points at work?

Common issues revolve around earnings, the tasks you get up to, the people you deal with and what you believe your title should be. Commuting times and how you are balancing your work and home lives are also important factors.

List the things that you would want to change. Then ask yourself: Are these issues going to be fixed by moving job?

It is possible that you will end up with similar commute times, similar working relationships (you don't know who you'll be working with until you get there) and the same processes dressed up in a different costume. Work out which of these things would make you happier if they changed. A pay increase is likely to fulfil you for a while, but we all end up living to our means and you are likely to only want more again in a few years' time. Not that this should stop you earning what you deserve – but money will not equal imminent job satisfaction.

4. RISK VS. REWARD

PROS AND CONS OF A NEW JOB

TYPICAL PROS AND CONS

When considering whether to seek or accept a new job, a solid place to start is a good old-fashioned pros and cons list. What are the positives and negatives of moving job? Be honest with yourself. Don't assume the unknowns – you can't always be sure that your boss will be better or that your workload will be less. If there are assumptions that need to be clarified, then pose these questions to both your current and your potential employer before committing to anything. You have to get these things ironed out in writing before accepting any contract. Your future self will be grateful that you have.

To get you started, here are some lists of typical pros and cons that come with a new job – but you'll need to make them specific to you.

The typical pros are:

- **Higher salary:** Research shows that when we move job, the average salary increase is 14.8%, while average wage growth (among people who stay in the same job) is much less, at 5.8%.[38] So it certainly pays to change job should money be your key motivator.
- **New job title:** A new job may allow you to change tack to a slightly new role or show your career progression from one level to the next.
- **New projects and learning opportunities:** Working on new things will grow your skills and understanding.
- **Better work–life balance or commute time:** You may be able to adapt your circumstances to fit around your life better.

Some typical cons are:

- **Probation period:** Most jobs come with a probation period, after which time either you or your employer can opt out of your contract. Having this trial period can cause uncertainty about the future – things might not work out.
- **Proving yourself:** In the first six months, any diligent employee will feel the need to show their aptitude. This can result in longer hours and more time spent getting to grips with new information, which may result in higher stress levels.
- **Unknown colleagues:** While you may meet some great new people, you might also be working closely with some questionable characters. You won't know until you get there.
- **Another promotion or pay rise will be a few years down the line:** Your next chance for a step up won't be for a while.

SCORECARD

After creating your own lists, see where you end up. Is there an obvious choice now that you've analysed the potential outcomes? If things are close, try putting a score out of 5 next to each item, with 1 being 'not that important' and 5 being 'very important.' You can then add up the scores to get a pros score and a cons score. This will allow you to see more minute discrepancies.

If there is anything you are unsure of, get clarity from the relevant sources and re-evaluate.

THOUGHTS AND RESOLUTIONS

5. NEW JOB DISSATISFACTION

YOU MOVED, AND NOW YOU'RE NOT SURE IT WAS THE RIGHT DECISION

PROMISE VS. REALITY

Check back against your contract. Is the job in hand not what was agreed on paper? You have the right to insist that the job you are undertaking is what you signed up for. If you were diligent, you would have set some of these issues straight before starting, so you have an agreement to point towards to set things straight.

Remember that a probation period is not just for the benefit of your employer – it is also there for you to decide if you like the job. You have every right to leave after this point, or at any point in fact.

ADAPTING

Can you adapt the role or your attitude towards it?

Pinpoint the issues that you have and take them to your manager – ideally with some suggested solutions, as this will make their life easier and show that you're keen to make it work. A good manager will look at what they can do to make the situation work best for you. After all, if you are a good employee, they will want to keep you. It costs an organization a lot of time and money to find someone new.

If you decide to stick it out for the time being, attempt to focus on the positives. These might simply be that you work closer to home and are therefore able to spend more time with your loved ones. Look at what you can reframe so that there is a positive to be found.

MAKING A MOVE, AGAIN

You may realize that you liked your old job a lot more than you thought! If you left on good terms, there may be the option to return. This will look good on your CV as it will show that you are valued and your ex-employer is more than happy to take you back.

It's also worth remembering that we all make mistakes and, with a valid explanation, future employers should understand. And if they don't? Then perhaps they aren't the right organization for you and you should look elsewhere.

PART NINE NOTES

HOW MUCH OF MY TIME DO I SPEND IN JOY?

IS IT THE JOB OR ANOTHER ASPECT OF MY LIFE?

ARE THESE ISSUES GOING TO BE FIXED BY MOVING JOB?

STAYING OR GOING SCORECARD

WHAT TO DO IF I DON'T LIKE MY NEW JOB

> **Every moment of discomfort is an opportunity for self-improvement.**

PART TEN

CONTINUOUS
SELF-IMPROVEMENT

1. PERSONAL PROGRESS

WHY IT MATTERS AND
HOW TO DO IT

Progression is demarcated by hitting business targets and helping the organization to thrive. What this doesn't take into account, however, is our own personal progression. There are plenty of skills that we learn as we go along that were way outside our knowledge base before we started. These should be celebrated, too. Presentation skills are a good example. Very few of us are taught how to design a story, create a digital version of it, and then get up in front of people and confidently and eloquently express ourselves. It takes a lot of practice for most people to get this right.

TAKE TIME TO REFLECT

Taking time to reflect is an incredibly powerful tool. The book *Dose* highlights a Harvard Business School study showing that "people who were given the opportunity to reflect at the end of a working day showed 20+% boost in efficacy (efficiency in performance) in subsequent weeks at work."[39] So, let's take some time to do this now.

GRADE YOUR OWN ACHIEVEMENTS

You know what feels daunting to you. Usually these are the things that you know you need to do but that make you feel a touch nervous, or require extra attention because it's the first time you're embarking on them. Notice when you feel that a particular activity doesn't come easily to you and applaud yourself when you undertake it. Don't shunt it to the bottom of the to-do list and never get around to it.

Acknowledge the character traits that come naturally to you and also those that don't. If you are quite extraverted, it may be that you know you need to actively listen more in order to respond appropriately. If you are naturally introverted, the idea of asking a colleague to collaborate on a project might feel really uncomfortable.

Stepping outside your comfort zone will build your confidence. Each time you achieve something that you found daunting, you will feel pride and satisfaction. This reward will encourage you to do these types of things again and again. Keep a record of your personal milestones so you can look back and feel bolstered by your achievements.

YOU ARE YOUR OWN HARSHEST CRITIC

Negative self-talk can become a liability if it becomes self-depreciating and starts to damage your confidence. Remember that it's very unlikely that anyone will be judging you in the same way that you are. Make sure you are compassionate with yourself.

2. POSITIVE SELF-TALK

THE POWER OF POSITIVE AFFIRMATIONS

In 2005 the National Science Foundation published an article reporting that we have 12,000 to 60,000 negative thoughts about ourselves each day – up to 80% of our total thoughts for the day. This shows that we're hardwired to focus on the negative. But this isn't helpful on a day-to-day basis, so we need to try to redress the balance.[40]

POSITIVE AFFIRMATIONS

Positive affirmations are positive statements that we say to ourselves. And, handily, they're completely free to create and use.

> "Affirmations can decrease stress, increase wellbeing, improve academic performance and make people more open to behavior change."
> (Christopher N. Cascio et al., *Social Cognitive and Affective Neuroscience*[41])

Self-affirmations help to bolster our sense of integrity. Through continued and persistent positive self-talk, we feel less threatened by an outside 'attack' on our character. When others make us feel a bit crap, we usually feel our sense of self is threatened. Voices in your head may ask, "Are they right?" or "What did I do wrong?" If, however, you are bolstered by a positive sense of self, you will feel more resilient to these threats and they are less likely to affect you negatively. You won't dwell on them and let them bring you into an unpleasant, and therefore unhelpful, headspace.

WRITE YOUR OWN

Start by writing out encouraging statements about yourself, all as "I am..." statements. These can be things that you've said about yourself or that others have said about you. An example is, "I am honest, intelligent and hardworking. This makes me an invaluable employee."

Then start repeating these statements to yourself, every day, so that they start to become your own personal mantra. Write them on post-it notes, save them as your screensaver or put them up on your fridge. The more that you see these words, the more they will become ingrained in you. By inputting positivity, you are drowning out the negative self-talk. Ideally, we want to have more positivity in our lives than negativity, creating an optimistic overall outlook on life.

A POSITIVITY PACK

When you are having a bad day, are feeling inadequate or know that you have slightly screwed something up (we all have days like this, no matter how brilliant we are), it's a healthy practice to take a moment to remind ourselves that we are well regarded and (most of the time!) good at our jobs.

Create a document and write down all the positive words you've been told, goals you've achieved, projects you're proud of and nice things people have said. Get into the habit of copying and pasting compliments that you are emailed and praise that you have received into this document. This will become your positivity pack. You can read it back any time that you need a confidence boost to drown out any negativity from the day.

THOUGHTS AND RESOLUTIONS

3. HAVE A PANIC SYSTEM

*CREATE A TOOL TO
TURN TO IN TOUGH TIMES*

PREVENTATIVE MEASURES

Have a go-to routine for when things get tough. When we're in a panicked state, it's helpful to have a system to turn to that will help calm us down. Having a pre-set routine means you don't have to think about what needs to be done when you're in a fight-or-flight state. When anxiety kicks in, it can be especially hard to think about anything other than our worries.

Think about what works for you. It could be going for a walk, putting on a good song and singing at the top of your lungs, or doing some restorative stretching or breathing exercises. Take a breath, step away and change the focus.

FOUR-PART BREATHING

A brilliant breathing technique to calm the nervous system is four-part breathing. Inhale through your nostrils for four counts, hold the breath for four counts, exhale for four and then hold the breath for four before continuing the cycle. If it helps, imagine a square as you breathe, using the four sides to visualize the steps.

It's said that US navy seals use this technique in combat to calm the mind. Not only does it take focus away from the issue, instead directing it to the count of your breath, but it also regulates your breathing. When we're anxious, we breathe quickly and in our chests rather than breathing more deeply, which includes the rise and fall of the stomach. The four-part breathing technique tricks your body into calmness using breath as the tool.

WORK OUT WHY

Once you've had a chance to settle yourself, take a moment to reflect. Take a look at the situation and work out why it didn't turn out the way you wanted it to. It may have been that you were tired and felt emotionally under-resourced, so your reaction wasn't as you'd want it to be. Consider how you can react in the future. Perhaps you were faced with a particularly unpleasant person. Create a plan for the next time you cross paths with that person, or anyone else who might rub you up the wrong way.

Every moment of discomfort is an opportunity for self-improvement. It's powerful to analyse what went wrong and why, and how you can react better in the future.

THOUGHTS AND RESOLUTIONS

4. GET A SECOND OPINION

THE VALUE OF COACHES AND MENTORS

MENTORING

Mentoring is a great way to acknowledge and analyse the challenges you face and to create a plan to untangle you from them. You will feel the relief of sharing your problems while knowing that you are actively working out a way to cope, and ultimately to develop.

A TRUSTED ALLY AND ADVISER

A mentor's purpose is to help you succeed, after discussing and deciding on the right path together. It is one thing to have family and friends to support you, and quite another to have someone in your corner whose job is to hear your issues and help guide you. They understand the business landscape that you are in and can pose challenging questions that your relations might not know to ask.

DISCOVERING MORE ABOUT YOURSELF

We rarely set aside dedicated time that is designed to reflect on our desires and actions. A mentor will ask you questions to help uncover your strengths and weaknesses – both those that you knew about and those that you didn't – and help you to mature these into valuable character traits that will help you to excel.

GOAL SETTING AND ACCOUNTABILITY

Having regular check-ins with your mentor means showing your actions as the weeks go by. Stagnation stops and progress begins. You become accountable for the goals that you set yourself. It's very easy to ignore our own goals if we are the only person who knows about them – but the very fact that you are investing time (and potentially money) with a mentor means you are dedicated to progress.

FINDING A MENTOR

Find a mentor who does not work with you every day so that they can be impartial and you know that they have yours, and not your organization's, best interests at heart. There are tons of ways to find someone who's right for you. Start with an idea of the things you would like to tackle – some personal objectives. You can then search for an area of expertise based on what you want or on your industry. Seek recommendations. Make sure you have a discovery call to see how well you get on. While we don't need to be best friends with our mentors, we do need to feel that we can trust and respect them. Remember that being 'triggered' (see *Part Four*) by your mentor isn't a bad thing – this may highlight some further self-analysis that's needed.

Mentors do not have to be paid. You might find someone that you admire who is willing to offer their time to share their opinions and help to direct you.

5. THERE'S MORE TO LIFE THAN WORK

FOCUS ON THE THINGS THAT MATTER

DEATHBED REGRETS

"I wish I hadn't worked so hard" is in the top five deathbed regrets, according to *The Guardian*.[42] Having written an entire book dedicated to how to handle your work life and progress, I feel it's important to remind you that work is only one aspect of your life, albeit a sizeable chunk. There are many other places that we can find happiness and satisfaction.

YOU ARE NOT YOUR JOB

You have the choice to define yourself as you wish. Your job doesn't have to have any part in that. If you *only* define yourself by what you do, I would encourage you to embark on some immediate and deep self-exploration to see what it is that you like doing, and are good at, outside your employment. You don't want to find that if your job disappears, you no longer know who you are and lose your purpose, which has been a common phenomenon among the retired population and is referred to as the "post-work identity crisis."[43]

DON'T COMPARE YOURSELF TO OTHERS

Everyone has been guilty of this at some point. Perhaps it's a colleague who keeps being praised and promoted, or a friend who appears to be storming their career. There will always be someone who seems to be 'doing better' than you. Social media enables us to portray the filtered version of ourselves that we want others to see and doesn't show the truths under the surface.

Don't look outwards to validate your self-worth.

YOU DESERVE TO ENJOY WHAT YOU DO

We deserve to enjoy our jobs. No job will be perfect – there will be challenges and tough times. You may have to reframe your perspective to find more joy than irritation in certain moments. But you don't want to be dreading your work. It takes up too much time for us to be living in drudgery like that. So take time to find something that aligns with your values as it will give you pride, satisfaction and, ultimately, enjoyment.

" Focus on the things that matter. "

PART TEN NOTES

PERSONAL PROGRESS I HAVE MADE

MY POSITIVITY PACK

MY PANIC SYSTEM

WHO COULD I TURN TO FOR A SECOND OPINION?

WHAT MATTERS BEYOND MY WORK?

NOTES

1. *Gen Z Spotlight Report* (Carson College of Business, Washington State University, 2021), accessed 21 June 2023, https://business.wsu.edu/bnw2021-genz-special-report.

2. "Values" (Oxford English Dictionary), accessed 21 June 2023, https://www.oed.com.

3. Christina R. Wilson, "What Is Self-Sabotage? How to Help Stop the Vicious Cycle" (Positive Psychology), last modified 22 April 2021, https://positivepsychology.com/self-sabotage.

4. "Over the course of a typical 50-year employment stint, almost a quarter of a person's time is spent at work." See "17 Remarkable Career Change Statistics to Know" (Apollo Technical), last modified 4 December 2022, https://www.apollotechnical.com/career-change-statistics.

5. Adam Morgan, *A Beautiful Constraint: How To Transform Your Limitations Into Advantages, and Why It's Everyone's Business* (Hoboken, NJ: Wiley, 2015), p. X.

6. "Integrity" (Merriam-Webster), accessed 21 June 2023, https://www.merriam-webster.com/dictionary/integrity.

7. Joe Palca, "Why Do We Get Annoyed? Science Has Irritatingly Few Answers" (National Geographic), last modified 11 December 2019, https://www.nationalgeographic.co.uk/history-and-civilisation/2019/12/why-do-we-get-annoyed-science-has-irritatingly-few-answers.

8. James Clear, *Atomic Habits* (London: Random House, 2018).

9. Antoine de Saint-Exupéry, *The Little Prince* (New York: Reynal & Hitchcock, 1943), p. X.

10. Chuck Ewart, "The Power of Planning" (US Chamber of Commerce Institute for Organization Management), last modified 18 June 2012, https://institute.uschamber.com/the-power-of-planning.

11. Rick Hanson, *Hardwiring Happiness* (London: Rider Books, 2013).
    See also Fit4D, "We Are Hardwired for Negativity so Have to Make Conscious
    Decisions to Focus on the Good" (Medium), last modified 8 August 2017,
    https://healthtransformer.co/the-neuroscience-of-behavior-change-bcb567fa83c1.

12. A. J. Adams, "Seeing Is Believing: The Power of Visualization"
    (Psychology Today), last modified 3 December 2009,
    https://www.psychologytoday.com/gb/blog/flourish/200912/
    seeing-is-believing-the-power-visualization.

13. "Stop Self Sabotaging Behaviors Worksheet" (Greater Minds), accessed
    21 June 2023, https://www.thelawofattraction.com/wp-content/uploads/
    Stop-Self-Sabotaging-Behaviors-Worksheet-1.pdf.

14. Alexandra Pope and Sjanie Hugo Wurlitzer, *Wild Power: Discover the
    Magic of Your Menstrual Cycle and Awaken the Feminine Path to Power*
    (London: Hay House, 2017).

15. Ethan Kross, Marc G. Berman, Walter Mischel, Edward E. Smith and
    Tor D. Wager, "Social Rejection Shares Somatosensory Representations with
    Physical Pain," *PNAS* 108, no. 15 (2011): 6270–6275.

16. Marcus Aurelius, *Meditations*, 7.47.

17. Amy Edmondson, "The Role of Psychological Safety: Maximizing Employee
    Input and Commitment," *Leader to Leader* 92 (2019): 13–19.

18. *Dealing with Difficult People* (Boston, MA: Harvard Business Review
    Press, 2018).

19. Gloria Mark, Daniela Gudith and Ulrich Klocke, "The Cost of Interrupted
    Work: More Speed and Stress" (University of California, Irvine), accessed
    21 June 2023, https://www.ics.uci.edu/~gmark/chi08-mark.pdf.

20. "Is Hybrid Working Here to Stay?" (Office for National Statistics), last modified
    23 May 2022, https://www.ons.gov.uk/employmentandlabourmarket/
    peopleinwork/employmentandemployeetypes/articles/
    ishybridworkingheretostay/2022-05-23.

21. Judith Orloff, *The Empath's Survival Guide: Life Strategies for Sensitive People*
    (Boulder, CO: Sounds True, 2018).

22. "Understanding Emotional Dumping and Healthy Venting" (Online Counselling Service), accessed 21 June 2023, https://www.onlinecounsellingservice.co.uk/emotional-dumping.

23. Julie Smith, *Why Has Nobody Told Me This Before?* (London: Michael Joseph, 2022).

24. "When You're Smiling, the Whole World Really Does Smile with You" (University of South Australia), last modified 12 August 2020, https://www.unisa.edu.au/Media-Centre/Releases/2020/ when-youre-smiling-the-whole-world-really-does-smile-with-you.

25. Kevin Duncan, *The Intelligent Work Book* (London: LID Publishing, 2020).

26. Mihaly Csikszentmihalyi, *Flow: The Psychology of Optimal Experience* (New York: Harper Perennial, 2008).

27. Monica Sharma, "Men More Likely to Ask for a Pay Rise Compared to Women" (HR Review), last modified 17 September 2021, https://www.hrreview.co.uk/hr-news/men-more-likely-to-ask-for-a-pay-rise-compared-to-women/137844. The survey, conducted by Censuswide in April 2021, surveyed 254 directors, senior managers and middle managers who contribute to the decision-making process in HR in companies of 250+ employees across the UK.

28. "Employers Reveal the Top Factors Preventing Workers' Chance of Promotion in New CareerBuilder Survey" (CareerBuilder), last modified 2 July 2015, https://press.careerbuilder.com/2015-07-02-Employers-Reveal-the-Top-Factors-Preventing-Workers-Chance-of-Promotion-in-New-CareerBuilder-Survey.

29. "Employers Reveal the Top Factors Preventing Workers' Chance of Promotion in New CareerBuilder Survey" (CareerBuilder), last modified 2 July 2015, https://press.careerbuilder.com/2015-07-02-Employers-Reveal-the-Top-Factors-Preventing-Workers-Chance-of-Promotion-in-New-CareerBuilder-Survey.

30. Crystal Raypole, "How to Identify and Manage Workplace Bullying" (Healthline), last modified 29 April 2019, https://www.healthline.com/health/workplace-bullying#What-is-workplace-bullying.

31. Isabelle Kirk, "How Many Britons Display Signs of Impostor Syndrome?" (YouGov), last modified 7 June 2022, https://yougov.co.uk/topics/society/articles-reports/2022/06/07/how-many-britons-display-signs-impostor-syndrome.

32. Isabelle Kirk, "How Many Britons Display Signs of Impostor Syndrome?" (YouGov), last modified 7 June 2022, https://yougov.co.uk/topics/society/articles-reports/2022/06/07/how-many-britons-display-signs-impostor-syndrome.

33. Ingrid Fetell Lee, *Joyful: The Surprising Power of Ordinary Things to Create Extraordinary Happiness* (London: Rider Books, 2018), p. X.

34. Stephanie Collier, "How Can You Find Joy (or at Least Peace) during Difficult Times?" (Harvard Health Publishing), last modified 17 October 2022, https://www.health.harvard.edu/blog/how-can-you-find-joy-or-at-least-peace-during-difficult-times-202210062826.

35. Ryan Holiday and Stephen Hanselman, *The Daily Stoic: 366 Meditations on Wisdom, Perseverance, and the Art of Living* (London: Profile Books, 2017), p. X.

36. "17 Remarkable Career Change Statistics to Know" (Apollo Technical), last modified 4 December 2022, https://www.apollotechnical.com/career-change-statistics.

37. Ali Francis, "Gen Z: The Workers Who Want It All" (BBC Worklife), last modified 14 June 2022, https://www.bbc.com/worklife/article/20220613-gen-z-the-workers-who-want-it-all.

38. Chris Kolmar, "26 Average Salary Increase when Changing Jobs Statistics (2023)" (Zippia), last modified 7 February 2023, https://www.zippia.com/advice/average-salary-increase-when-changing-jobs.

39. Dulcie Swanston and Iain Price, *Dose: Personal Prescriptions for a Happier Life and 52 Science Based Ways to Get it* (Walsall: Top Right Thinking, 2023), p. X.

40. National Science Foundation.

41. Christopher N. Cascio, Matthew Brook O'Donnell, Francis J. Tinney, Matthew D. Lieberman, Shelley E. Taylor, Victor J. Strecher and Emily B. Falk, "Self-Affirmation Activates Brain Systems Associated with Self-Related Processing and Reward and Is Reinforced by Future Orientation," *Social Cognitive and Affective Neuroscience* 11, no. 4 (2016): 621–629.

42. Susie Steiner, "Top Five Regrets of the Dying" (The Guardian), last modified 1 February 2012, https://www.theguardian.com/lifeandstyle/2012/feb/01/top-five-regrets-of-the-dying.

43. Ron Carson, "How to head Off a Post-work Identity Crisis" (Forbes), last modified 7 September 2021, https://www.forbes.com/sites/rcarson/2021/09/07/how-to-head-off-a-post-work-identity-crisis

BIBLIOGRAPHY

Atomic Habits, James Clear (London: Random House, 2018)

A Beautiful Constraint: How To Transform Your Limitations Into Advantages, and Why It's Everyone's Business, Adam Morgan (Hoboken, NJ: Wiley, 2015)

The Daily Stoic: 366 Meditations on Wisdom, Perseverance, and the Art of Living, Ryan Holiday and Stephen Hanselman (London: Profile Books, 2017)

Dealing with Difficult People (Boston, MA: Harvard Business Review Press, 2018)

Dose: Personal Prescriptions for a Happier Life and 52 Science Based Ways to Get it, Dulcie Swanston and Iain Price (Walsall: Top Right Thinking, 2023)

The Empath's Survival Guide: Life Strategies for Sensitive People, Judith Orloff (Boulder, CO: Sounds True, 2018)

Flow: The Psychology of Optimal Experience, Mihaly Csikszentmihalyi (New York: Harper Perennial, 2008)

Hardwiring Happiness, Rick Hanson (London: Rider Books, 2013)

The Intelligent Work Book, Kevin Duncan (London: LID Publishing, 2020)

Joyful: The Surprising Power of Ordinary Things to Create Extraordinary Happiness, Ingrid Fetell Lee (London: Rider Books, 2018)

Why Has Nobody Told Me This Before? Julie Smith (London: Michael Joseph, 2022)

Wild Power: Discover the Magic of Your Menstrual Cycle and Awaken the Feminine Path to Power, Alexandra Pope and Sjanie Hugo Wurlitzer (London: Hay House, 2017)

ABOUT THE AUTHOR

With over 15 years of experience, Rosie has worked in all corners of the communications industry, including creative agencies, media agencies, production companies, digital agencies and media owners.

She has 19 industry awards to her name, one of which is the world-renowned Young Cannes Lions Award – winning Silver – which was the first time the UK won a place in its 20-year history.

She has been a top biller in creative partnerships at Metro newspaper and worked in partnership with Google. She is co-author of the international best-selling book, *The Excellence Book*.

After a decade of the corporate life, she set up on her own so that she could work with companies that agreed with her values – specifically those in mental health and health and wellbeing. She now consults several mental health focused research departments at King's College London as well as mentoring small businesses and individuals.

Contact the author for advice, training or mentoring at
www.ZansProductive.com

BY THE SAME AUTHOR

£9.99/$12.95
ISBN: 978-1-915951-07-6